PERMISSION TO
DREAM

PERMISSION TO
DREAM

CHRIS
GARDNER
AND
MIM EICHLER RIVAS

AMISTAD

An Imprint of HarperCollinsPublishers

HarperCollins books may be purchased for educational, business, or sales promotional use. For information, please email the Special Markets Department at SPsales@harpercollins.com.

FIRST EDITION

Designed by Nancy Singer
Illustrations by Noa Denmon

Library of Congress Cataloging-in-Publication Data has been applied for.

ISBN 978-0-06-303156-2
ISBN 978-0-06-309974-6 (ANZ)

21 22 23 24 25 LSC 10 9 8 7 6 5 4 3 2 1

AUTHOR'S NOTE

In this work of narrative nonfiction I offer an account of an actual journey I shared with my nine-year-old granddaughter—a memorable day in both of our lives. Although the highlights of that experience are faithfully recalled, I have taken a few liberties in rendering certain details used to describe people, places, and conversations that happened along the way. This approach allows me to honor the oral storytelling tradition handed to me by my elders. In that time-honored style, I get to pass the torch, offering parables and lessons that form my philosophical guide to "happyness" (misspelling intentional). My aim is also to re-create the actual dreamlike quality of that day, one that befits a subject as universal as the permission to dream. A few of the strangers depicted on our journey are composites of many of the fellow dreamers I meet every day. They are the working folks in every public-facing industry, and the students, audience members, peers, and others who reach out to me with questions every day and in almost every setting. While conversations recalled herein are not intended to be word-for-word reenactments, they have been thoughtfully recalled in the true spirit with which they were spoken.

CONTENTS

PROLOGUE

ATOMIC TIME— HOLLY'S GIFT

Sometimes—perhaps at what might seem to be the absolute lowest point in your life—you'll be given a key to the most rewarding, powerful dream possible. Maybe it's a dream you've never even considered before. That key may arrive in the form of a question you are asked by the one person you love too much to ignore.

Some years ago such a question was put to me by Holly Norwick, my lover, best friend, and patron saint for over two decades. We had not married, but there was never a doubt about our devotion to each other. She was mine and I was hers. When Holly and I started seeing each other in the late 1980s—at a time when she was one of very few women working in the upper echelons of Wall Street—we connected as kindred spirits. We were both dreamers in pursuit of becoming world-class in our professional lives.

Let me correct that. Holly was world-class in *everything* she did. Cooking was no exception. She loved to cook. And when I say world-class, I'm talking the Rembrandt of risotto, the Michelangelo of meatballs. Aretha Franklin was the Queen of Soul, but Holly was the Queen of Soul Food! Our deal was she would make me anything to eat at any time of day as long as I did the dishes. Seemed like a good deal to me. Besides, I had help with those dishes, or at least with the pots. Cassius, our handsome boxer, who thought he was a child, did the pots. He had this process of sort of *stabbing* the pot that had been used to cook the meat sauce—so he could then lick it clean. All I had to do was rinse!

One year as a Christmas present I managed to surprise Holly with her dream kitchen, which had taken me two years to complete. Working with a top design team, we completely rebuilt the old kitchen, first by raising the counters, which had been too low for her, and then by adding all the latest bells and whistles. Her world-class dream kitchen put Wolfgang Puck's to shame. To say that I went all-out would be an understatement.

When she first saw her kitchen, Holly cried so hard she couldn't speak.

"Why are you crying?" I had to ask, and she said it was because she was so happy she couldn't imagine ever feeling that happy again. That led in part to my misspelling of "happyness"— the *y* is there as a stand-in for *you* and *your* dreams and *your* definition of what makes you happy. Long after *The Pursuit of*

Happyness came out as a book and a film, I continue to misspell it to honor the *y* in "Holly."

No matter how hard we worked, Holly was my partner in fun, turning the smallest of occasions into memorable celebrations. Every now and then we'd set aside time to get as far off the grid as possible. We were blessed beyond our dreams, in more ways than I could count.

Everything was cool.

Or so I thought. That is, before the day I woke up and smelled the coffee—figuratively speaking—and had to confront alarming news.

Actually, when I woke up that day and heard Holly say, "Good morning," in her usual upbeat, irresistible voice, I probably had too much on my mind to detect her worry. Everything felt important: changes at the company I'd founded twenty years before; the reviving economy, full of challenges and opportunities; work on my second book; an increasingly busy travel schedule as speaker and business consultant; and, on a happy note, the fact that Chris Jr. had recently become a dad, making me the proudest of grandfathers.

That day, when I opened my eyes and heard her wish me a good morning, I was happy to still be under the covers. In that foggy state of debating whether it was time to get up and go to the gym or to grab a few more z's, I sort of rubbed the sleep from my eyes and looked over at Holly, propped up on a pillow. I smiled. But wait—was that a worried look on her face? Then she said softly, "I've got to tell you something."

Fully awake, I sat up.

Whatever else she said I don't recall, only the words "I'm losing my vision."

My initial reaction was to immediately go into denial mode—where I basically spent the next three years. "What do you mean you're losing your vision?"

This made no sense. She looked perfectly healthy and fine, as she always did. Even just having awakened, Holly was stunningly beautiful, graceful, elegant, and obviously athletic—the picture of health by any definition. She was only fifty-one years old.

Holly looked at me and winced, clearly anxious.

My mind raced. "Do you mean you need new glasses?"

But it was the way she had said the words "I'm losing my vision" and the look of fear in her eyes that had already let me know this was well beyond my small-minded question. I can see now that was my first step—a big old leap, in fact—into a place called Total Denial.

As Holly began to explain herself, I cut her off with a sudden realization that marked the first exit off Denial Highway. "Wait a minute." I reminded her of the trip she'd just taken from Chicago to see her parents. "You just drove to Arkansas and back. Why didn't you tell me this before?" Not allowing her a chance to answer, I went on: "If I'd known this, I wouldn't have let you drive down there!"

"I know," Holly responded. "That's why I didn't tell you."

We had just gone Beyond the Wall—not a welcoming place at all. Everything that is uncertain lies Beyond the Wall.

Swinging into action, I made phone calls. My response was to take charge, get to the right specialists, and solve the issues. Any number of problems could have been the main cause for her apparent loss of vision. Having an eye issue myself, I first sought answers from my own doctor, one of the top ophthalmologists in the world, Dr. Theodore Krupin at Northwestern University's Northwestern Memorial Hospital. Having a fair amount of reach and access has its advantages. I used every connection available in the field of medicine. Holly and I went together to a series of visits with the best medical specialists in the world. I didn't know then, but figured out quickly, that one of my jobs was to declare, "We've got this! We're going to be fine!" If you've ever been down this road with someone you love, one of the FIRST things you learn is how not to show that you're scared too.

Initially, we learned that Holly had been slowly losing her eyesight due to an inoperable but benign brain tumor that was tangled up in her optic nerve. When an experimental protocol called proton radiation therapy looked promising, we went for it, commuting together from Chicago to Bloomington, Indiana, for five days of treatments every week for six weeks. The theory was that the proton radiation would target only bad cells and not harm the good cells. At the time, only five facilities in the country offered these treatments, and we felt blessed that we had the access and the resources to obtain the best medical help.

At this point in my life I was more in demand than ever as a public speaker, on pace to be traveling two hundred days a year for at least the next decade. But when the doctors informed us they had an opening for Holly to begin this treatment, I looked at my calendar and for the first time in years I had *no* place to be and *nothing* to do for six weeks! I accepted this as God's way of saying, *No, son, it's not that you don't have anything to do. It's that your job NOW is to take care of Holly.*

So Holly and I, along with Cassius, traveled weekly to Bloomington for those six weeks, then drove back home for the long weekends. The Three Amigos, 2.0.

During our free hours, Holly and I continued to work as diligently as ever, maintaining a sense of normalcy. We watched old movies and I read aloud to her every night—proving that a medical ordeal can be a good opportunity to catch up on books, TV, films, and music. Holly—who loved music even more than I do—knew the names and lyrics to every song in the world. We made the most of every minute together. Cassius approved.

One of the many lessons I learned during this period with Holly and with Cassius was that I would have made a good dog. Maybe that's because I've got this thing about loyalty. If you've been there for me, I'm going to be there for you!

The treatment bought us time, an asset I now understood as the most precious in the world. You never appreciate it until you lose it. You got money and you lose money? You can make some more. You got time and you lose it? You can't get it back or make more of it. It's gone.

Holly used her time to run her company, cook in her beloved kitchen, and still enjoy and savor our adventures to favorite destinations together. But as her vision began to go completely, a series of falls and other mishaps led to a new diagnosis: the tumor, once benign, was stage IV brain cancer. Instead of my constant reassurance that everything was going to be fine, all I could say now was "I'll be here, right here with you all the way!" Sometimes the most important thing you can do for someone you love is to have them really *know* you'll be there.

Don't know what the doctors are going to say? *I'll be there!*

Don't know what that MRI is going to say? *I'll be there!* Don't know what that x-ray is going to say? *I'll be there!* Just being there will become the most important and precious and honorable thing you can, and will, ever do in your life, and it won't feel like it until you get way down the road.

We both knew that there was only so much time left on the clock of Holly's life and our lives together, even if I refused to accept it. Months later, after another series of falls and a second round of brain surgery and an extended hospital stay, I was able to bring her home. After signing the release forms and loading up the car for the drive home, Holly smiled at the recognition of the first song to come up on our playlist: Quincy Jones's "Comin' Home Baby"!

Around the time of our last Christmas together, I bought Holly the wristwatch that had been on her wish list. It wasn't especially fancy or expensive, but it had a black face with white lettering that she liked. When she opened up the box and put the watch on her wrist, I'll never forget how she said with a kind of enchantment, "Oh man, look—it's got Atomic Time."

"Atomic . . . what?" I laughed and had to look at the watch to see what Holly meant.

That's when it hit me. Because she had lost her sight completely in one eye and was only seeing partially with the other eye, she could only make out a part of the word. In fact, the clockface read AUTOMATIC TIME.

She was right in one sense: the only way to make sure you're living fully, engaged in the passionate pursuit of your dreams, to the absolute nth degree, is to live in "Atomic Time." Even after discovering the watch kept "Automatic Time," she loved it more because she still saw it as measuring atomically—a method by which, to her mind, every second should matter and be prized, every single particle of time valued.

Denial soon became impossible. Holly was running out of time, even if I still refused to accept it. Every moment, every thought and conversation took on a new sense of urgency, and it seemed as though she always wound up asking me the same question: "Now that we can see how truly short life can be, what are you going to do with the rest of your life?"

Holly understood that I had stopped dreaming. The very thing that had given me power and purpose had failed me. Or I had failed it. I was not in a space to dream because the thought of a future without her was unbearable. My fear was too great. As the beneficiary of, witness to, and recipient of too many blessings to count, too many miracles and manifestations of good, I couldn't face the reality of life without her.

Holly refused to give me permission NOT to dream. She wasn't going to let me off easy. In my memory I can still see her confined to bed, unable to move most of her body on her own. With the little sight left to her, on one of her last mornings, Holly called me over to ask the same question about how I planned to spend the time that was left to me.

Words failed me. I took a deep breath but was lost.

She was not having my silence. "Tell me," Holly insisted, asking again, "what are you going to do with the rest of your life?" She was not going to give me a pass to fall apart. She was telling me in so many words—*What are you going to do when I'm not here? Because I'm not going to be here to see it, you have to tell me what you're going to do.*

Holly took away my excuses and demanded that I figure it out so that I could live in "Atomic Time" and reclaim my own permission to dream. She gave me my marching orders to write this book and to answer the question that I was not able to confront until later events took me on a most unexpected journey.

Wherever you are in your life, I hope this story reminds you of the power to dream that lives in each and every one of us. My hope is that it helps you to embrace the energy of Atomic Time. To know that every second matters. To know that you matter. To know that what you dream and pursue can matter. We all have witnessed in our collective journey of the present challenging moment that circumstances can change radically in an instant. We each have to do a hard pivot toward new and changing terrain. We control only our dreams and our pursuit of them. That's Holly's gift I want to share with you.

You can change your life in a snap if you live in Atomic Time. How? By choosing to transform your *one day* into *today*. The first step to creating that reality comes with the courage to move past your fear and go Beyond the Wall.

Give yourself the permission to dream. Let's go!

ONE

OUR GREATEST EXPORT

A top-of-the-line harmonica—that's all it took to change my life in two days.

This was a few years back on a winter morning in Chicago that was so cold it must have broken every record. Despite the foreboding gray sky and biting wind, my granddaughter Brooke and I ventured out into the freezing rain, already mixed with light snow, so I could make good on a promise to get her what she had told me was the harmonica of her dreams.

Yes, a harmonica. *Of her dreams.*

Brooke, nine years old at the time, seems to have arrived in this world with an uncanny and sometimes unnerving knowingness. That quality shows up in many first grandchildren, I'm told.

Something else about a first grandchild is they can be that one person on the planet who believes you are a real-life SUPERHERO!

My granddaughter, the Honey Bear, thinks that I, Poppa Bear (as she calls me), am the Black Panther! Who am I to argue?

Brooke had tested her thesis a couple of years earlier. In the process, I learned—or relearned—something about how each of us can actively pursue happyness, simply by taking our dreams out for a test drive.

* * *

"Poppa, got a minute?" Brooke had begun our phone conversation in the soft, sing-song lilt of a seven-year-old. She rarely called when I was on the road, so I suspected this was important.

"For you, I got all the time in the world," I answered, moving fast toward the gate where my flight was starting to board.

In the years since Holly had been gone, I'd kept busy, working, traveling, always on the move. The work was satisfying, but I had yet to answer how best to use however long or short the time left to me.

Brooke, clearly warming up to ask me something important, remained casual. "So, whatchoo doing today?"

"Nothing, just getting on an airplane to go to Malaysia."

"Oh! Malaysia's far! You can call me when you get home."

I told her that whatever was on her mind, I was all ears.

Brooke: Well, Poppa, I was thinking . . . You know the president, right?

Me: Yeah . . .

Brooke: Good. I want you to call him up.

Me: You mean, just call him. For what?

Brooke: Well, I want you to tell him that I'm coming to
the White House and I want to take a picture
sitting at the Big Desk!

Me: Let me see if I've got this right. You want me
to call the president of the United States and
tell him that my seven-year-old granddaughter
wants to take a picture at his desk?

My granddaughter corrected me. "Tell him that I am seven
and a half."

I almost said out loud *Well, that's going to seal the deal* but
thought better of it.

One of the nice things about getting into your sixties, is that
you are old enough to know better, and still young enough to say,
"Well, why not?" And I made the call.

By the time I returned from Malaysia, I had received a call
back from the White House staff, saying, "Come on down!"

Brooke's dream to sit at the Big Desk to see how it felt surpassed her greatest expectations. She and the president got on
famously.

I will never forget how, before my granddaughter and I said
goodbye to President Obama, she gave the place a last once-over
and nodded, as if to say, *I'll be back.*

I have no doubt.

There you have it. At age seven and a half, Brooke had given
me a refresher course on having the audacity to dream. She gave
herself permission to *ask* for an opportunity to check out a dream

and try it on for size. The dream was a big one, but the act of dreaming was natural to her, as fundamental as breathing. She began with the proposition of *one day*: *One day I could be president.*

The proposition of *one day* is a guiding principle that says we live in a country that, at least in theory, has bestowed on each and every one of us the right of self-determination—to grow up to be and do and achieve our highest aspirations. This, I believe, is also the essence of what makes the American Dream our greatest export.

In recent years, as I've traveled to well over eighty countries and all the continents (with the exception of Antarctica), I've come to the absolute conclusion that our homegrown dream has gone global. We should probably start calling it the Universal Dream because it exists outside language, culture, religion, or politics. In my travels, I've also seen how we've neglected aspects of it that once made us the envy of the world. There have been moments when I've even begun to feel we may need to import back our greatest export—to reboot the promise of equal access for all to life, liberty, and the pursuit of happyness.

Brooke didn't need permission to dream. She gave it to herself. At age seven and a half, she wanted to go to the White House and sit behind the Big Desk and see how it felt. For her, it was a fit. Like looking through a long-distance telescope and seeing herself in that future picture.

The next year the focus and seriousness of her dream to *one day* hold the highest office in the land only grew. Before long, she began to plan her roadmap to 1600 Pennsylvania Avenue.

Every now and then I'd have to commend Brooke for maturity. She'd look back, in all confidence, and agree, yes, "Eight was great!" Now that she had enjoyed another birthday, however, she would have to add, "But nine is *fine*."

* * *

Ironically, it was almost easier to get Brooke into the White House than it was to find a time to go out and get her this harmonica she was so intent on having.

Oh yeah, she was so excited about getting a harmonica that when asked what all she wanted for Christmas, that was IT. From the moment when my son Chris Jr. arrived on New Year's Day to drop Brooke off, that's all she talked about. Had I found the right store? Did I know which one to buy? How soon could we go?

Of course I had scoured the town and queried all my contacts in the music industry before being told about a well-kept secret, some hole-in-the-wall shop that catered mainly to professionals and collectors. The only problem was that they had sketchy hours and, frankly, were located in a sketchy neighborhood.

"Listen," I explained to Brooke, "they're open tomorrow. We'll have a good breakfast, bundle up, catch a cab, and get there right when they open. Deal?"

She nodded solemnly before adding, "I may not be able to sleep tonight."

Brooke's passion delighted me, even if she couldn't say where this new interest came from.

In the past, whenever someone would ask me, "How will I know if I've found the thing I'm supposed to do that will lead to my happyness?" I'd usually bring up the sleep test. By that I mean, if something captures your imagination so much that you can't wait for the sun to come up so you can get out and pursue it, it's likely to be more than a passing fancy. Something about the dream, small or large, should just click when you first give your-self permission to dream it—like a key that fits into a lock and opens a door to possibilities. Or like sitting at the Big Desk in the Oval Office at the White House and having it feel good.

My hunch was that Brooke was being very strategic about learning to play music. She seemed to understand that she proba-bly could become proficient pretty fast on a small instrument like a harmonica and then graduate to bigger and better instruments. To the best of my knowledge, she had no specific inspirations or genres—like the blues—that she wanted to master. It did occur to me that somehow Brooke thought it would be cool to pull out a harmonica and wail on it.

Come to think of it, so did I!

Whatever had lit that fire in her, it didn't matter. All that mattered was that if my granddaughter wanted a harmonica, then, no questions asked, we were going to get her the best—even if it meant having to travel Beyond the Wall to get it.

Yep, turns out that in all of Chicago, my hometown for the last thirty years, the one place where you can get the best harmonica is this music store on the North Side, way up in a neighborhood that's practically uninhabitable. And that's what I mean about going Beyond the Wall. If you're a fan of *Game of Thrones*, like me, you know about the frozen world that the Knights of the Watch have to defend against with the zombie-like Whitewalkers at large and threatening humankind. If you don't get the reference, no problem. All you have to know is that nobody wants to go Beyond the Wall. Definitely not on January 2nd in bad weather.

You might be thinking, *How bad could it be? You live in Chicago, weren't you used to it by now?*

The answers are "Really bad" and "No." You forget sometimes how bitterly mean and intense the cold can be. Besides that, the weather report had not predicted any precipitation, even suggesting milder than usual temps. But, nope, the minute Brooke and I rushed from my apartment lobby into the waiting cab, a burst of wind, thick with ice and snow, huffed and puffed at us like a killer zombie appearing out of nowhere.

Settling into the cab, Brooke laughed, held up her hands that were swaddled in thick mittens and rubbed them together. I laughed too but instantly regretted having been so cavalier in my attire. Brooke, thanks to her mom seeing to it that she had come to Chicago well prepared for inclement weather, was dressed appropriately. Not me. Somehow I'd decided to wear a sweater topped with a fashionable but lightweight car coat and a wool scarf. No hat, no gloves.

When I announced the address of the store to the cabdriver, he looked surprised—or was it concerned? Yet he didn't say a word as he pulled out onto North Wabash and headed toward North Michigan Avenue, where he swung a left to veer north. From here it was a straight shot for a while, almost to the edge of the city, then a bit farther west and north to the general area where Brooke's harmonica could be found.

Even with the heat in the cab, we could see our breath as we exhaled.

"It's winter all right," I said, making small talk. "In full force."

"Good thing we're not walking!" Brooke added.

The farther we drove, the fewer people there were out on the street. Those we did see looked like moving snowmen and snow-women as they pulled their clothes tight around themselves and leaned forward, heads down, so as not to be knocked over.

The icy rain and snow appeared to be sticking to the ground. Our driver responded by slowing down, for good reason. Without saying anything, I did wish he'd pick up the pace, maybe get us there faster so we could return to the warmth and safety of home.

Along the lake, the epicenter of the Windy City, the cold is famously brutal. Due to a complex set of factors, related to latitude and longitude and wind vectors, possibly it's the cold-est spot in North America. Maybe the cold is not as harsh as Antarctica but it's comparable. My granddaughter—who lived in Boston with her mom most of the year—was right that it was good we weren't out there walking. Been there and done that. When the wind comes driving across the lake at you, it feels like you've traveled to the North Pole—like you really should have stayed home and ordered in.

All I'm saying is, contrary to the weather prediction, this was a cold-as-hell day. The kind of day that makes you wonder why you live in Chicago.

"Poppa, is that where the Cubs play?" Brooke asked, at which point our cabdriver piped up and told her that was, in fact, Wrigley Field we were passing.

As the two of them began to discuss who had the rowdiest fans—Chicago or Boston—it occurred to me that part of why I avoid going Beyond the Wall has to do with Cubs fans who celebrate wins and losses equally hard. And those festivities al-ways involve alcohol. So much so that during, before, and after the regular season, almost everyone in the vicinity is some type of inebriated. Most games are specifically held during the day in the hopes of curbing drunkenness at night. Instead, fans drink all day. In other words, you can expect trouble Beyond the Wall.

Then again, the more I thought about it, maybe—just maybe—instead of finding trouble, or instead of nothing memorable happening at all, it was possible that Honey Bear and I were off on a bold and exciting expedition.

*   *   *

We got lost.

The cabdriver overshot the music store on Clark and then had to double back. Traffic had been thinning considerably, and there was almost no one driving or out walking in this cold. Our driver tried rerouting a couple of times on his GPS, but it kept directing us onto streets we didn't want to be on even inside a cab. There wasn't much to do but surrender to the situation.

Brooke, nine-year-old future president and harmonica enthusiast, sensing perhaps that I could use something to distract me from worrying that our adventure was not off to a great start, decided to use the time to ask me questions.

Her favorite line of questioning drew out stories about her dad as a little boy and about my life when I was growing up. From as far back as I can remember, Brooke also has had a special connection to her great-grandmother, my late mother, who died years before I became a grandfather.

Bettye Jean Gardner Triplett—or Moms, as I used to call her—was the one person in the world responsible for instilling in me the permission to dream. She herself, the daughter of a sharecropper, born in Little Rock, Arkansas, and raised deep in the heart of Louisiana in the darkness of the Great Depression, and under the heavy hand of Jim Crow, never had the opportunity to realize her own dreams. And yet, when it came to her children, she refused to be prevented from making every sacrifice necessary so we would have the choices she had been denied. The gospel according to Bettye Jean, handed right to me, was never to let anything or anybody keep me from my dreams of doing whatever, and being whoever, I so chose.

Brooke remembered there was a story she hadn't heard in a while about the time I wanted to play the trumpet—not so different from her wanting to learn the harmonica. The details were blurry so she asked to hear it all again.

"Why'd you wanna play the trumpet, Poppa?"

"Because Miles Davis played the trumpet, and I wanted to be Miles Davis."

"You wanted to play like him?"

"No, my biggest dream, my life's mission, was to be a world-class jazz musician. Not to be like Miles but to be him." The first time I ever heard a record by Miles Davis, I explained, the minute my uncle dropped the needle onto the LP, after five notes I thought that a wizard had cast a spell over the whole room.

Brooke had heard about vinyl records from her dad—my son, Chris Jr., a music lover himself—but she knew nothing about the difference between 45s (the little records with big holes) and LPs (the big records with little holes). I had to stop myself from telling my granddaughter why new music technology is inferior to how recorded music sounded back in my day.

The last thing I wanted to do was be one of those old guys sitting up on the porch talking 'bout *Back in my day* . . . Instead,

I recalled for Brooke how happy it made my mother when I expressed a desire to learn to play music.

Moms moved heaven and earth for me to get a secondhand trumpet and lessons with the best local teacher she could find. I studied music and music theory, and played that trumpet for nine years.

Telling my granddaughter the story brought back those days in vivid detail. I learned to play like a pro. I learned to inhabit the soul of jazz. I memorized every note of every Miles Davis composition. I even started talking like Miles.

Brooke rolled her eyes at that point.

"Yeah, that's how your great-grandmother reacted too. And that's when she sat me down and gave me The Talk."

Brooke gave me a quizzical look. As in *Go on*.

"Your great-grandmother sat me down at the kitchen table and said, 'Baby, you're pretty good with that thing, but you can't be Miles Davis. There ain't but one, and he already got that job.'"

Well, as I went on to tell Brooke, that confused me at first because my mother had always told me I could do and be whatever I wanted. Only the hitch was, I had to do it as Chris Gardner—not as Miles Davis. The reality I had to face next was that at eighteen years of age, Miles was in New York City, playing with Quincy Jones and Dizzy Gillespie. Changing music forever. At the same age, I was in Milwaukee, Wisconsin, playing with a couple of guys named Pookie and Ray Ray. We were good but nowhere near world-class. We were not anywhere close to changing music.

"But you know what, Brooke?" I said, coming to a new discovery, "those nine years of playing trumpet and wanting to be Miles taught me to be ready when a bigger dream came along."

She thought about this new twist on the story that she hadn't heard before. Then I watched as a question appeared on her face and kind of burst from her. "Poppa, when you were younger did you have any other dreams?"

"Are you kidding me? All the time!"

At this, our cabdriver laughed, and pulled up right in front of the music store. "We all dream," he admitted, backing me up.

Brooke, not quite satisfied with my answer, had to ask a follow-up. "But, Poppa, what else did you dream that was *important* to you."

The question suddenly took me back to a point in my adolescence—a hard time—when I was twelve, thirteen, and older. Out of the blue, memories came at me, falling like the rain and snow outside our cab, of learning how to practice dreaming. This was something I had really forgotten. In those days, to get out of the house, which was dominated by a violent, abusive stepfather—worse than any of the scary stuff that goes on Beyond the Wall—I would go and just sit outside the Greyhound bus station in downtown Milwaukee.

Every detail had imprinted itself in my recollections—how those flashy big Greyhound buses would load up passengers all looking so happy to be going places that to me were worlds away. My uncles, my mother's brothers, had all served in branches of the military and had told me stories of their travels. The possibility that one day I too would leave and go see the world and travel to all those exotic places was the ongoing dream that sustained me, fed me, and kept me warm inside.

At the Greyhound station, I embraced the American Dream— our greatest export. With the Dream came a promise that I could build a future for myself, one that would take me further than I could envision at the time. Every departing bus had a destination indicator up above where the driver sat. I memorized the route numbers of all the destinations—Kansas City, Cleveland, Detroit, Saint Louis, and more. The names of those cities conjured livelier and richer dreams the more I imagined visiting those places. *One day.*

Most of the time, I didn't have a dime in my pocket, and I certainly couldn't afford a ticket. But the dream of being able to *one day* pay to get on a bus and go somewhere different and new—wow, that was everything.

As I told Brooke about how much the Greyhound station had meant to me, I couldn't help smiling. From an almost forgotten dream of *one day*, now these many days and adventures later I couldn't count how many countries I had visited in the past ten years alone. Eighty something?

And here we were, outside our destination Beyond the Wall, and it felt like we had traveled forever all in one day to get here. Now all we had to do was make our purchase and turn around to go back home.

Having bonded with our cabdriver, I paid the fare and gave him an extra twenty dollars to keep the meter running. He didn't look thrilled but said he'd wait.

"Fifteen minutes," I promised, and with Brooke following me out of the cab, we hustled as fast as we could, careful not to slip, as we made our way toward the entrance to the music store.

TWO

ONE DAY . . .

My head down, I kept an eye on our feet as we crossed the icy sidewalk toward the elusive musical instrument store. After all the effort, I'd started to doubt its existence. Other than a faded plaque with a store name and address on the building itself, obscured by encrusted snow, there were no signs in the darkened windows announcing the type of inventory inside or even if it was an actual store. The only way to enter the place was through a flimsy set of double doors. Whoever had installed them must have had something against tall people.

That's when it dawned on me that the store might be closed on account of the weather. The thought made me glance back to make sure our driver was still waiting. To my relief, the cab was right there, though shrouded in a mist of freezing rain and falling snow. Reassured, I reached for the handle of the entry's double doors, half expecting it to be locked. Brooke ducked under my arm, pushed through, and led us into a cavernous, otherworldly dreamland.

My granddaughter and I took two or three steps into the store before stopping to gaze around in awe. Out of the darkness of that grim winter's day, we fell into the warm embrace of an amber-lit expanse overflowing with musical instruments, equipment, accessories, and more. From acoustic to electric to digital, this had to be the mothership.

We scanned the vision in front of us: from floor to ceiling, up stairways, down aisles of shelves and long sections filled with all kinds of instruments. Signs announcing different departments pointed this way and that, to our right and to our left. So much for a hole in the wall. As far as I could tell, this originally must have been one store that had spilled over into the next store, and the owners had invested in real estate rather than an outside remodel.

Now I understood why this place had come so highly recommended. It was the Shangri-La of tools for making music. If Keith Richards were in town and in need of a guitar string, he would come here. If Drake wanted to freestyle and have a recording session, he could have set up here. Not fancy or highbrow, just an institution that had been in business forever, it reminded me of a musical instrument museum. After further scouting around, I came to the conclusion that the place had instruments that no one alive had ever played. But if you asked for it, they would get it out from under lock and key just for you.

Clearly they catered to a professional, serious clientele but also to newer musicians, coming in for the most recent model of a digital keyboard or drum kit or gizmo for making beats and all the latest DJ setups of ones and twos for clubs or house parties. They had all the stuff the old-school guys and gals needed, all the stuff the new-school guys and gals needed, and all the stuff that would let the newer players sound like the older players.

When you think of a kid in a candy store, man, that was me. I couldn't help but get revved up, pointing out a top-of-the-line trumpet polished so shiny it looked more like gold than brass. Then I spotted the Gibson and Fender Rhodes guitars, and "Oh, that's a VOX amp, Brooke! See how big it is?"

She nodded with admiration and amazement.

"In the olden days," I told her, "if you needed an amp you had to bring one in that was like that—as big as a refrigerator—to get a certain sound." We looked over at the newer options. "See, today amps can be the size of a toaster and you can still get that same huge sound."

Pretty much everything was either represented or in abundance—string and wind instruments, all the different percussion instruments, keyboards of every price range, both electric and acoustic, guitars of every sort, and all the various accessories, like violin bows, reeds for saxophones and clarinets, music stands, instrument cases, metronomes, tuning forks, conductor batons, and a vast array of instruction books and sheet music.

All around the store different instruments were being played or tested, not in concert but still in spontaneous harmony—a Latin beat on some conga drums, an island groove on a marimba, a jazz riff on a stand-up bass. Some prodigy started to warm up on a piano, maybe with Chopin. Someone else began to tune a guitar.

I was in heaven. My granddaughter reminded me of Dorothy

in Oz—with an expression that read, *We ain't in Kansas no more, Poppa!*

We'd landed in the company of a handful of folks who, like us, must not have gotten the bad-weather memo. With so much sound, you would have thought the store was crowded, but as Brooke and I continued our tour, I realized there were far more salespeople in here than customers.

The closer my inspection of these salespeople, the more convinced I was that we had walked into a time warp. Without question, the salesmen and women had been employed by this store a *lonnnnnggg* time. For lack of a better term, they were from back in the day. There were a lot of long shaggy beards, wire-rimmed glasses, balding heads, and graying afros, and a couple of saleswomen were dead ringers for Janis Joplin and Tina Turner—only forty-five years later. Kind of like hippies who had grown up and become grandparents but were still hip. One salesman, helping a more youthful customer in the guitar section, had some of the latest adornments—a ponytail, beads, bracelets, and tattoos—but the tattoos were not so new. You could tell by the sagginess of his skin.

Something else that struck me about the employees was that they were all dressed for the weather—lots of plaid shirts, sweaters, turtlenecks, and hiking boots. Unafraid to face the elements, they appeared to have come to work with the same sense of meaning and purpose as any crew who drove snowplows or worked on power grids. Then again, this could be just how they normally dressed—as if they belonged more in Portland, Oregon, than in Chicago. Or like they had set out from Portland in the late 1960s, walked across the country, made a stop at the Woodstock festival, and wound up randomly here in Illinois.

Whatever their actual stories, the salespeople were obviously devoted to helping customers choose the musical instruments of their dreams. Their expertise and passion added one more layer to the charm of the store.

Mindful of our schedule, I led Brooke over to the salesman with the ponytail and tattoos, who had just brought out a guitar for an enthusiastic customer. The handoff was incredible. The young man took the guitar, already in its carrying case, and held it as though it were a baby he was adopting. Was this the biggest dream come true of his life, having that guitar? Maybe not. But small dreams lead to bigger ones, and he had the appearance of someone whose life would change thanks to that guitar.

Brooke's eyes sparkled. She was about to get her dream harmonica. The salesman spotted her anticipation, leaned over, and said to the both of us, "Be right with you. I just have to check something in my catalog for this dude here." The customer with the new guitar nodded graciously.

The sight of our sales guy flipping through a catalog triggered something inside me that I couldn't place at first, bringing with it a wave of emotion that caught me off guard. For a few seconds, I was lost in that wave.

* * *

Where do dreams begin? How do we give ourselves permission to dream when the reality of what we see and experience all around us in our everyday lives offers little hope or reassurance that our dreams can ever become real?

For me, permission to dream began with the Spiegel catalog and my older sister, Ophelia. Starting when I was almost three, and up until the age of about five and a half, Ophelia and I were separated from our mother for different intervals as she tried to flee Freddy, our violently abusive, homicidal stepfather. At one point, trying to put the money together to get the three of us to safety somewhere else, Moms got into legal trouble.

For a time, Ophelia and I were put in foster care together. During that year and a half, before hard memories were formed, I used to have a dream about the prettiest lady who would come to the foster home and make candy for me—just syrup in a pan. The dream turned out to be real. Much later in life when I re-counted that dream for my mother, her eyes filled with tears as she explained, "That lady was me, baby." She had been able to get out of jail on leave a couple of times, for long enough to go visit her children.

After one such visit, Moms managed to convince her older brother and his wife—Uncle Archie and Aunt TT—to take in both me and Ophelia together. To the best of my recollection, I was four and my sister was six. While I don't remember who made up the game that we called This Page/That Page, I can see us as if it were yesterday, sitting together for hours, sometimes sprawled on the rug, going through the entire contents of the Spiegel cat-alog, starting on page 1. We had a contest that began when you flipped a page and whoever could put their hand on that next page first could claim all of the items pictured there. Everything.

We claimed women's dresses, jewelry, men's shoes, kid's sleepwear, hats and coats and suits. Socks, underwear. Most of what was in the Spiegel catalog were items you'd find in department stores. We dabbled in other catalogs, like Sears Roebuck, which gave us access to camping equipment, power tools, and lawn mowers. And there were bicycles and trampolines, and special toys you couldn't get anywhere else.

Whoever touched that next page first would have to say, "That page is mine!" If it was me, I might add, "*All of that* is mine!" We also took turns, not wanting all this ownership to be lopsided. And if the items pictured on a page weren't of interest, then we could take a pass and the other person could claim two pages in a row. Why not? The act of being selective was also empowering. Choosing the right page and the right stuff, hey, that was part of the game.

We were two little kids who had nothing, other than the love and comfort of our aunt and uncle at that time, and the necessities of life, but no material things. The concept of ownership was in fact so remote that the act of claiming goods on the pages of a catalog was our way of having some sort of superpower. That was how I began to dream that there would come a time, *one day*, when the items in This Page/That Page would really and truly belong to me. So did Ophelia.

But then, somehow, without discussing it, the game changed, such that when one of us hit a page, we had the power not just to dream of having things for ourselves but to dream of giving to the other. Now, that was big!

"All this," I'd say to my sister, "all this is yours." And Ophelia would hit a page and tell me, "I'm giving you all this. One day all these clothes and shoes will be yours." My sis and I gave each other all kinds of things from catalogs. I seem to remember for her birthday I gave Ophelia a page with chainsaws, jackhammers, and a metal work shed. She gave me sets of dishes and some kitchen drapes. Everything. No matter how far off in the future our *one day* happened to be, our gifts to each other were still so appreciated and so real in our minds. The feeling never left me—*One day all this is going to be mine, and one day I'm going to give you all of this stuff too.*

The memory of those generosities made me grin as I stood in the middle of the music store. Apparently young dreams die hard, because I went on to have a serious clothes and shoes habit. The thought has also occurred to me that Holly's kitchen was an adult realization of This Page/That Page. Dreams really do begin at an early age, at stages in our lives when we may not even be conscious of them.

* * *

My momentary escape into the past—not much longer than half a minute—came to an end with the sound of Brooke asking, "Poppa?" As soon as she had my attention, she said, "You looked like you were seeing something invisible. A ghost or something."

No one had ever said that to me except for my mother. That sent me off on a split-second memory wave again.

As a little boy and later on, whenever I had to take myself emotionally out of the difficulties of the present moment, I would think hard about how much better it would be in the future. Moms would notice this and ask, "Son, you seeing them ghosts again?"

To which I'd always answer, "Yes."

And Moms would always say, "That's okay, son. As long as you're seeing them with the eyes of your soul, no one's got to see them but *you.*"

In later years, whenever I thought of her telling me this, it would summon the line of scripture (Heb. 11:1) that says, "Now faith is the substance of things hoped for, the evidence of things not seen." There are some excellent lessons in the Bible that my mother tried to reinforce. I wish I'd paid more attention in Sunday school. Luckily I had Moms trying to prepare me for a world that she may have felt was beyond her reach but that she dreamt for me. She actively chose to reassure me that it was okay to peer into the future and imagine possibilities.

In my memory I could hear her saying it was okay to see ghosts. It was as if it was yesterday, starting from the time I was not quite six. This was when Ophelia and I were finally reunited with our mother—who had decided the only way for us all to be together was a path of least resistance with Freddy. If she tried to leave him, he would kill her and us. As hard as that may be to contemplate, for anyone who has grown up in an escalating cycle of domestic violence, that's a fact. Maybe that's also why I learned early to give myself permission to dream—to *survive*.

"Yeah, I did see a ghost, come to think of it," I admitted to Brooke, "and it reminded me of a game I used to play with your great-aunt Ophelia, my big sister."

When I explained to Brooke how This Page/That Page worked, and how it made us just as happy to give a whole page of stuff to each other as it did to claim it for ourselves, I added, "I remembered something else too. What do you think the difference is between a wish and a dream?"

Brooke wasted no time in answering. She was nine, after all. "That's easy, Poppa Bear," and then she reminded me of the Harry Potter books. "A wish is something you want to come true with magic."

Oh, right. I gave her the look that said, *Go on.*

"And a dream is something you make happen."

"Ah," I said and asked, "so are you saying that you have to choose your dream wisely?"

Before Brooke could answer or we could continue on that topic, our ponytailed salesman was finally ready. He ambled casually over. "And what can I help you two find today?"

Brooke took center stage and replied, "A world-class harmonica!" She even said it with a hand on her hip and a wave of her head.

That's when I realized this whole expedition was not in my control at all but a dream my granddaughter definitely had chosen to make happen.

"What kind of world-class harmonica did you have in mind?" the salesman asked, his bracelets and beads jangling as he looked at me rather than my granddaughter.

After I set him straight that it was Brooke who was in need of a top-of-the-line harmonica, and that because she was a beginner, we'd need an excellent instructional book, our salesman corrected himself.

"So . . . world-class you say?" He began to list different models of harmonicas they carried.

Brooke, unsure, repeated the phrase "world-class" and then gave an example, saying, "You know, the red Ferrari harmonica."

Wow. She had heard me tell that story a few times. It came from the point in my life when I'd decided not to pursue music and also not to use the training I'd been given in the US Navy to become a heart surgeon or medical research specialist. This was the story that had led to finding my way instead to a career in the world of Wall Street that spans the field of financial services. And it was all on account of a red Ferrari that caught my eye one afternoon in San Francisco.

The truth is, of course, the gleaming fire-engine-red Italian sports car was *not* what sold me on Wall Street. Not for a minute. It was a flash across the screen of my life giving me the opportunity to check it out, and prompting me to ask two of the most powerful questions that anyone can use at any time. On a day in my late twenties when I was just coming to terms with the fact that I was not able to support a girlfriend and our baby on my medical equipment sales job, I happened to see a guy about my age pull up to a valet and hop out of this dream car. The words came wailing out of my mouth like I was Miles Davis blowing on the trumpet: "Hey, I gotta ask you two questions!"

He kept walking, almost ignoring me. Well, we're all in a rush. I was too. But *I had to know.* I maneuvered myself to stand in front of him while still being respectful and giving it up to his obvious success. Whatever I said next I don't really remember, but my subtext was *Hey, I know you gotta run, but first, please, you gotta tell me something, you gotta solve this mystery, man. This could be my lucky day and yours too!*

He slowed down and waited for my question.

"What do you do?" I asked first, followed up quickly by "And how do you do it?"

What do you do? And *How do you do it?* Those questions can be used by anyone at any time whenever you are in search of that thing that engages you to the *n*th degree.

Those were the two questions that helped me find my dream, the thing I wanted to be world-class at doing. And by world-class

I mean that when you speak of any particular field—any given arena or calling—if that is your field your name will be on everyone's list. World-class.

The owner of the red Ferrari answered me straight. He was a stockbroker who worked at the San Francisco Stock Exchange. How did he do it? To show me, he was willing to take me onto the trading floor that same week. And the moment when I arrived, it was like the key had been given to me. No matter what obstacles stood in front of me, I had *no* doubt about entering the financial services business because I could FEEL it. It was the same feeling I had listening to Miles Davis the first time—the energy in the air of the stock exchange was electric, another world. On that stock exchange floor, I knew this was where I was supposed to be. Not *I think I can.* Not *I'd like to try.* It was *This is where I'm supposed to be.*

As soon as I had found my key, the trick was then to find the right door into my place in that world. Of all things, it was a world-class sports car that had gotten my attention and helped me find the right dream for me.

Now Brooke was asking for her own world-class sports car of harmonicas. I shook my head with pride. But then, not wanting to waste any time, I jumped in and elaborated, saying, "Right, the best you got. We want the harmonica that Stevie Wonder played, you know, like on 'Fingertips, Part 2.'"

At first the sales guy kind of shrugged, his face blank, as if to say, *Who would know that?* I didn't want to insult him by suggesting he Google it. Then, however, miraculously, a gleam came into his eyes.

"I was there!" He went on to tell us that on a night in 1963 he went with his parents to the Motortown Revue at Chicago's Regal Theater, where that song was recorded live. In the 1960s, there were two iconic concert halls for every Black artist dreaming of fortune and fame or who was already famous: the Apollo Theater in Harlem and the Regal Theater on the South Side of Chicago. The better known of the two was the Apollo. Its audiences were notoriously tough and would boo you offstage if you didn't knock 'em out in the first few minutes. The Regal, aptly named for its opulent design, was not as famous but was twice the size of the Apollo. And Chicago audiences were spoiled by the *best* of the blues and jazz artists, who were all local. So for the up-and-coming artists of Detroit's Motown, they could have easily been vicious.

On my 45—the small records with the big holes—the crowd roars when twelve-year-old Little Stevie Wonder starts to play the harmonica, on a song that is basically an instrumental. There is some singing—"Everybody say 'Yeah'!"—but no lyrics to write home about. Apparently, Motown producers came up with the melody of "Fingertips" to showcase Stevie's harmonica and bongo playing. When I heard it as a nine-year-old kid, I thought the producers were tricking us and had other people in the band playing harmonicas too. That's how amazingly full the harmonica sound from Stevie was. The historic moment in the song happened when ostensibly he was finishing up and went into a fast riff of "Mary Had a Little Lamb" and the audience went *craaaazzzzy*, calling for more. As the story goes, the band changed musicians for the next artist (whoever it was), but Stevie decided to come back onstage and play "Part 2." One of the band members who had just sat down, called out, "What key? What key?" and it ended up on the live recording.

"You know what's interesting about that?" our salesman related to Brooke. "It was real and people loved it." They loved it so much, he said, "Fingertips, Part 2" climbed to the top of the pop chart and made Stevie Wonder the youngest artist to have achieved that distinction.

For my granddaughter, this lore was mesmerizing. But we had been in the store a good ten minutes and didn't want to push our luck. We had a waiting cab outside to catch.

The salesman was now clear about just which harmonica to bring out: a chromatic (versus a more common diatonic) harmonica. Folk music players like Bob Dylan mostly play the diatonic, which has ten holes, but artists wanting a full organ sound, like Stevie, use the chromatic, which has as many as sixteen holes and a slide that can raise the pitch of each hole and add almost a vibrato. Our guy did warn us that the chromatic was harder to learn to play and would require more advanced breath control.

No problem. We wanted a harmonica just like Stevie had used on his biggest hits. And we were able to purchase the Hohner Chromonica Super 64 plus an instructional book. While the package was being wrapped, I remembered to tell Brooke about seeing James Brown in concert in Milwaukee when I was eighteen years old—at a cost of one dollar—in a massive auditorium connected to a state fair.

"Hmmm," Brooke mouthed. "Who is James Brown?"

Oh, that got me going. *Who is James Brown?* Prince and Michael Jackson rolled into one. The greatest showman, entrepreneur, songwriter, record producer of his day. James Brown sang and wrote songs that are as infectious today as they were forty-some years ago—"I Feel Good!," "Cold Sweat" (Parts 1 and 2) and so many more.

Women went *bananas* for James Brown. He had that massive, contagious energy that was irresistible. In telling her about the first big concert I attended, I could vividly recall that energy.

"For a dollar you had to sit up in the rafters. The show starts. And by the time James gets to doing 'Please, Please, Please' to close out the show, I'm in the front row! He gets all worked up and emotional, and he looks like he can't live without this woman in his song, and his people come and cover him up with this flamboyant cape all covered in sequins. Drama to the hilt!"

Brooke gave me her look: *Go on.*

"So I think the show is over, but then *bam*, he throws off the cape and gets back on the mic. Everyone is *on their feet*, begging right along with him—*Pleeeaaassee!* And a lady jumps up onstage, grabs the cape, and throws it out into the audience. We all got down on that cape like rats on cheese. The little piece I was able to hold on to was just a scrap, but it had pink sequins on it. I took it home and gave it to your great-grandmother, and she cherished it."

Just then our salesman returned and handed Brooke one of the store's plastic bags, which held her dream harmonica, carefully protected in a case, along with her instructional book. He shook my hand and thanked us for making the trek in spite of the weather. We bundled up, bracing for the cold. To my relief, we had succeeded in getting out of there in fifteen minutes exactly. But before we headed back outside, Brooke asked what it was about James Brown that made me like him so much, and I realized that it was because he was independent, never someone to play by the industry rules. He owned his own masters, did his own promotion, and started a label. Other artists, especially Black artists, were often exploited by their labels to sell tickets and records, but they were barely compensated. Not James Brown.

When she asked me what my favorite James Brown song was, it came immediately to mind: "I Don't Want Nobody to Give Me Nothing." I talk-sang a few of the lyrics as we ventured into the frozen northern tundra. "I don't want nobody to give me nothing. Open up the door, I'll get it myself."

The snow and rain seemed to have paused. That was a good thing. But the temperature had dipped even lower. That was bad.

And when I looked toward the curb, our cab was gone. That was really bad.

THREE

AN UNDERGROUND RAILROAD

Brooke and I glanced quickly at each other, then back at the store, almost as though we were checking to make sure it hadn't vanished, and again at the curb where the driver and his cab had disappeared seemingly in a puff of icy mist. Apparently, even sitting in his cab up here Beyond the Wall had freaked him out and he'd decided to split—with the extra twenty dollars.

Trying not to be annoyed, I put a protective arm around Brooke's shoulder, thinking I'd flag down another cab and we'd be on our way again soon.

Guiding us quickly toward the curb, my head rotating

back and forth to catch any sight of a taxi, I was impressed by Brooke's ability to match my stride. Did I mention that this little girl—a naturally gifted basketball player—had recently enjoyed a growth spurt and was already tall for her age? That should have come as no surprise given the fact that her daddy is six foot eight and, the last time I checked, *still* growing. At eighteen months, Chris Jr. had been so huge and talkative and advanced, he often was mistaken for a three- or four-year-old.

That's how I remember him as a toddler in the early 1980s, when—through a complicated yet all too common set of circumstances—I became a single father and joined the invisible class of Americans I call the white-collar homeless. These were (and increasingly are) the untold numbers of women and men who go to work every day yet still can't afford a place for themselves and their families to live. White-collar homelessness was new in the 1980s, at a moment in history when, according to social historians, the definition of who could be classified as homeless began to change. These were people who had gone to school, studied diligently, played by the rules, and worked hard, only to lose their footing in a changing world.

In the early '80s, some of the leading causes of the explosion of homelessness included deep funding cuts to mental health and drug addiction programs, a major spike in the cost of living (especially rent), housing shortages (which included a sudden lack of safe rooms to rent in boarding houses), and a recession that lasted close to two years. The inner city had been in decline for a while, and that steamrolled into the '80s with folks trying to get out of the city and into the suburbs as well as new efforts at urban renewal that resulted in gentrification of certain safe, comfortable, middle-class neighborhoods into expensive, exclusive areas. Families of color, along with immigrants and lower income populations, were increasingly pushed out. Add to all that HIV/AIDS, which would claim San Francisco as its ground zero.

For many years, I heard from experts who estimated that as much as 25 percent of homeless adults had part-time or full-time employment. By the Twenty-Teens the percentage of homeless individuals who are employed or partly employed has risen to as high as 60 percent. One explanation for this dramatic increase has to do with the unprecedented number of single mothers and self-supporting women who do not have homes for themselves and their kids but who go to work each day for considerably less money than their male equivalents.

For most of the octane-fueled, *Star Wars*–driven, high-rolling 1980s, homelessness wasn't a topic making headlines or coming out of Washington, DC. Yet in pockets of San Francisco—where I'd visited my first trading floor and was trying to gain a foothold in the financial services business—the number of folks who had begun to fall through the cracks ought to have been alarming.

Being out in the elements with my granddaughter reminded me of those weeks and months without an address to call my own. That had been one of the rainiest winters in the Bay Area, breaking records set over a hundred years before. No matter how well I tried to protect Chris Jr. with a makeshift tent made of dry-cleaning plastic over his stroller, after hours of pushing my little boy and all our worldly belongings up the San Francisco hills, the wet chill had felt like something I'd never shake.

Whenever my son has been asked what he remembers of that

time, he recalls looking up through the plastic tent. "All that I remember," he would say about it, "is every time that I looked up my father was there."

The recollection caused me to glance down at Brooke just as she paused to look up at the sky. Under her arm, squeezed close to her body, was the waterproof bag that held her dream harmonica and the instruction book. With her free arm raised, Brooke lifted her hand, palm up, in her mitten, to see if there was any precipitation coming down.

"Well? Seems like it's stopped," I said, willing it to be so.

Ice crystals fluttered down. Brooke shook her head and pointed at the snow flurries starting up all over again. She craned her neck as she studied some darkly ominous clouds.

At least the brief break in the storm had been enough of a reprieve that there were more cars out on the street than earlier. But after some minutes of holding my arm up—poised to flag down a cab—I had to face the reality that there was not a taxicab to be seen.

My next realization was that the snow—wet and sticky—was definitely falling again. No icy rain mixed in with it.

You don't expect to be in a city like Chicago and go far without seeing a cab. Then again, it had been years since I'd been anywhere near this part of town, if ever, and it finally dawned on me that I had somehow been protected from the modern age of transportation. Uber had clearly changed the world.

"You know, Honey Bear," I said, beckoning her to follow me, "looks like the taxis have yielded this turf to Uber and Lyft. Whadya say we look for one of those?"

She nodded with relief as I pointed us in a southerly direction.

Brooke asked, "Don't you have to send them a text on your phone or something?"

"Whoa," I said, half joking, half not. Who knew anything about a text on a phone? This tech stuff was way above my pay grade.

Acting like it was no big deal, I egged Brooke on to join me in outpacing the snow. We walked at a fast clip for the next block or so, at which point the clouds began to drop rain, wimpy at first, then dotted once more with ice, which comingled with the snow. Not a welcoming sensation. And by now I was sure this was the coldest day of the year.

However, I did not want my granddaughter to have our otherwise successful expedition turned into an ordeal. My job was to prevent her from having to worry and to get us home fast.

We continued south—because I generally knew where we were headed—and I kept my eyes peeled.

Brooke, missing nothing, saw me looking over my shoulder and asked why.

"There may be a cab after all or one of those Ubers or Lyfts," I explained. Keeping my tone upbeat, I reassured her, "I'm just trying to get us out of here."

What do you know? As soon as I put on my cheerful voice, an Uber appeared out of nowhere, pulled up next to us, and dropped off a gentleman, who yanked his coat over his head and jogged off down the block. The Uber driver sat for a moment, checking something on his phone, I guessed, and I grabbed for the door handle, hoping to get his attention.

I could almost feel the heat inside the car. The door wouldn't open, though. Just then the driver rolled his passenger-side window down and leaned toward us, saying, "I got another pickup. You know you have to download the app."

"What? I don't have the app. Can't you just give us a ride?"

"Sorry!" he mouthed after rolling up the passenger window, revving his engine, and speeding off into the falling snow.

Why didn't I have the *app*? Never needed it. Note to self: *Gotta get apps. Gotta keep up with the times. Gotta stop thinking "Back in my day" is going to cut it for today.*

As if that wasn't enough of a wake-up call, at that same moment my cell phone elected to die. Not enough charge.

In the meantime, all I could think to do was continue walking and not give up hope that the right good-hearted driver-for-hire would appear. Only the Lord could have counted how many years I'd preached to myself and others that when you're in a tight spot, the Cavalry Ain't Comin', so you need to take decisive action. Remembering my own advice, I decided that if worse came to worst, we could bus it. There had to be a route somewhere in the vicinity.

To pass the time and stave off an acknowledgment of how cold it really was, I asked Brooke, "Did I ever tell you about the three most important decisions I ever made in my life?"

"No," she said, excited, "never."

"Well, I think you already know one of them."

"You said your dream was to be world-class at something! And so you decided to be a stockbroker, right?"

"See, now I'm impressed. You didn't even know there was going to be a quiz." There was another dream we had been talking about earlier, I reminded her. "Any ideas?"

Stumped, Brooke furrowed her brow, thinking deeply. Her

pace accelerated the harder she thought. Soon she started to grin. "You wanted to ride a Greyhound bus and travel to cities you'd never visited."

"This is too easy. Yes, right again, Honey Bear. My dream was to travel the world, and that's why I decided to join the Navy."

I skipped the details, telling her why joining a branch of the armed services was the only option available so that I could leave Milwaukee in a hurry. But it occurred to me, for the first time ever, how my dream of one day seeing the world had saved my life. It was the only insurance I had against not being killed by Freddy or getting thrown in jail for his murder. For too long he had beaten and battered Moms within an inch of her life. For too long he had stampeded me with a loaded shotgun pointed at my face, maddeningly ridiculing me for being the son that no daddy wanted. One time he pointed the shotgun at me as I was taking a bath, forcing me to get up and go outside the house, wet and buck naked, into the Wisconsin snow on Christmas morning.

In desperation, one afternoon after leaving a movie theater, where I'd just seen Jack Nicholson in *The Last Detail*, I decided to stop by the Navy recruiting office. There was something about his role as a sailor in that movie, plus the fact that I liked the uniform, that drew me in. I'd heard the radio commercials and the recruiting slogan many times, but that afternoon, when I saw their poster in the recruiting office window, I felt that the universe was speaking to me. JOIN THE NAVY, SEE THE WORLD, it beckoned. And that was it. My dream was going to save my life!

I enlisted on the spot and was soon *not* on a Greyhound bus but on an airplane, for the first flight in my life, on my way to the US Navy boot camp in Orlando, Florida—a world away. The fact that my uncles had each served in the military was an added incentive. When you've recently graduated from high school, the idea of public service or sacrifice of any kind may not be as motivational or meaningful as it later may become. At the time, though, the decision felt personal, on account of the influence of one of the people I loved most in the world.

I told Brooke, "My uncle Henry, the youngest of my uncles, he was my guy, the one who introduced me to Miles Davis, and the coolest thing of all, he would take me fishing out on the Mississippi River and tell me stories about being over in Korea and the Philippines and Japan." He would talk about the food and the beautiful women, *vividly*. More than anything, though, I never forgot how he showed me the globe of Planet Earth and spun it, telling me it was okay to close my eyes and pick a spot, and then go. And he also taught me the saying "The world is your oyster. It's up to you to go find your pearl." Here was the Navy, telling me I could do that.

The temperature in Chicago seemed almost to rise as I summoned images of those humid afternoons out on the boat with Uncle Henry, floating under the hot sun and waiting for a fish to tug on one of our lines. Never in my life, before or since, have I experienced that feeling of peace, not having to hurry or worry. It was the perfect setting for dreaming whatever I wanted to dream about the future. Some of the biggest thrills of my young life happened when we were cutting fast over the wakes of other boats, bouncing all over the place, and I was up in the front, throwing my hands up in the air, like I was the commander of a massive Navy fleet.

"Wasn't that dangerous?" Brooke asked when I described it.

"It was," I admitted. "That's why Uncle Henry had insisted that I have swim lessons before going out on the boat with him. The truth is that he couldn't swim very well. Nor could my other two uncles. And that's why none of them went into the Navy."

"Oh, you did it just to be different?"

"Aw, you know me too well." I laughed. But then came the hard part. Brooke asked if Uncle Henry had been extra proud when I signed up for the Navy. "Well, that's the sad thing," I said, but I had to pause to relive the shock of the news I had been given when I was only eight years old. Uncle Henry, as close to a dad as I had ever known, died one terrible afternoon on the Mississippi River after trying to swim out to retrieve the boat, which had not been docked properly. The undercurrent had been especially strong at that moment and just took him down.

To this day, I curse that river. It changed my life, robbing this world of Henry Gardner long before his time.

My granddaughter understood how the loss must have felt to an eight-year-old. She didn't try to find the right words. Brooke just shook her head and patted my back. Some losses you never completely get over, although I like to think that we can keep those loved ones alive in our spirit and in our actions.

Brooke changed the mood by asking, "Poppa, wasn't there one other important decision you made when you were young?"

"Absolutely," I said. "It was the first and most important of them all. And you know what, Brooke? If not for that decision, you might not even have been born."

She seemed somewhat skeptical.

I was serious. After Ophelia and I had moved back in with Moms and Freddy, when I was still five years old or so, I decided that the best way to not feel too sad about not having a daddy was to begin to dream about the daddy I would become when the time came to have children myself.

Ophelia's real father had moved to Milwaukee, along with my uncles, and he had stayed in the picture, showing up with presents for her now and then and even sometimes for me. But my real father was nothing more than a name Momma mentioned once or twice, a married man she had known briefly before leaving Louisiana to join her brothers.

As young as I was, I had some opinions about right and wrong. To me, at five years old, nothing could have been more wrong than abandoning your son or your daughter. I told Brooke, that's when I decided that "when I had a son of my own, I was going to be there for him. He was gonna know who I was, and I was gonna be in his life."

She thought about it and pondered something, asking me, if that was more of a dream or a decision.

"How'd you get so smart?" I couldn't help smiling, because it was a dream AND a decision. More than a decision, it was a promise. If we ever escaped wandering out here lost in the blizzard, I told her, she would win some kind of prize for being so sharp. That is, once we made it to the Promised Land.

* * *

Some dreams change. Some dreams are lost, forgotten, or abandoned because we're afraid or because circumstances beyond our control throw up obstacles or because we find another dream that gives us a greater sense of purpose. Some dreams are only in the moment, almost like a prayer that gets us through a rough passage or that lets us send concern and well-being to someone we love. Some dreams evolve and some are replaced. And some dreams are so powerful they refuse to let us go. Those are the ones that shape decisions and can even become promises that define not only our lives but also the lives of our children and grandchildren.

The American Dream was born of our ancestors' fervent hopes that their descendants could grow up to prosper in a free and fair land. Just as we dream for our children, my ancestors and yours dreamt of a future for us that many could never fully attain in their lifetimes.

Whenever I think of many of our ancestors, I'm reminded that we in America are the largest, most populated migrant nation of the world. Most everyone who came here did so in one of three ways:—Change, Chance, or Chains. Many came for a *Change*, for the want of religious autonomy or to escape the tyranny of a monarch. Many came by *Chance*, perhaps employed as a sailor on a ship that had not intended to come to shore here at all, or they came to stake out a claim in one spot but ended up in another spot, having crossed mountains, deserts, and oceans. And many, like my ancestors, were brought here from Africa in *Chains*. Not by choice.

Aside from our Native American ancestors, who were here long before anyone else, that's how we *all* got to America. It was Change, Chance, or Chains. *Period*.

For those who came in chains, to be sold on auction blocks, separated from family and from all familiarity, I imagine the only way to prevent their spirits from being broken would have been to dream. In four hundred years of slavery, as I have read, the most cherished dreams were not necessarily of going home again.

Many had been born en route to America or while their parents were already enslaved. They must have dreamt instead of a home they had yet to make in a place where they would be free.

How on earth could they turn that dream into a reality?

If they managed to become unshackled, they had to travel on foot and to learn to follow a map in the stars. Instructions came through coded spiritual songs, and they were sustained by imagery taken from the Old Testament and the story of the Israelites breaking free of bondage in Egypt, traveling on foot to the Promised Land. The Bible describes it as the Land of Milk and Honey—which turned out to be a dream too. No milk, no honey. Just more *desert*. Now they had real work to do to eventually bring forth a Garden of Eden out of a desert. But how else could they have kept going without the dreams of how much better it was going to be when they made it?

For any enslaved person who ran away, only a dream of something better could help combat the fear of punishment should they be found, captured, and returned. And the road to freedom was unmarked and treacherous. Maybe in your study of US history you learned about the passage of the Fugitive Slave Act of 1850. At that time, Congress passed a series of bills to placate Southern politicians, who were angry about the efforts to abolish slavery and had begun to threaten secession. One of the bills was this Act, which required all citizens—including in all free states—to capture runaway slaves. Anyone assisting runaways would be fined a thousand dollars (thirty thousand dollars in 2021) and put in jail for six months.

The Fugitive Slave Act would remain on the books through the beginning of the Civil War and not be officially and finally repealed until 1864, almost two years after President Lincoln's Emancipation Proclamation, which abolished slavery in the states that had seceded from the Union. The Fugitive Slave Act repeal took place about a year before June 19, 1865—the date those of us who know this history celebrate as Juneteenth—when 1,800 federal troops arrived in Galveston, Texas, to ENFORCE emancipation, finally and effectively ENDING slavery in the United States, two and a half years after Lincoln's proclamation.

Imagine the courage it must have taken for those among our enslaved ancestors who, in defiance of the Fugitive Slave Act, dreamt of escape and took action. The decision to try to go it alone, on your own two legs, or on horseback, or however you could travel by night so as not to be seen, had to be powered by dreams. It was also powered by the knowledge that others had done it and survived, having made it by following secret routes known collectively as the Underground Railroad. Along these routes were established way stations—homes, farms, barns, places where a friendly face offered food and water, wooded areas with supplies left in hidden places, even the occasional inn where temporary shelter and a place of refuge could be found.

Throughout my history dissertation, the Chicago snow had continued to fall, along with the temperature. Yet each time I glanced over at Brooke to gauge how she was doing, I detected a knowing gleam in her eye. Whenever I paused, she would look at me sternly with that same expression that said, *Go on.*

Still, just to make sure, I thought to ask, "Any questions?"

In fact, she had a question, she admitted. "Are you saying that our ancestors were not scared because they had their dreams?"

"No. You will still be scared when you're running for your

life. Courage is when you keep going, even if you're scared. Their dreams kept them going at those times when they must have felt they couldn't go another step."

Brooke and I talked next about how our ancestors could well have dreamt of a future in which a Barack Obama would become president of the United States. And, I added, they could have dreamt of a woman president too—like her.

She smiled and nodded, as if to say, *Well, yeah, I already knew that.*

* * *

Just as our expedition to purchase Brooke's harmonica had taken a few unexpected turns, I couldn't help but remember how my dream of joining the Navy and seeing the world led to its own plot twists early on. In spite of my grand vision of sailing off to all those places my uncles had described and other exotic locations, the farthest my Navy service ultimately took me was North Carolina—where I was stationed for the duration of my service. That was the first shock.

The next surprise was that, thanks to a job I'd once had, working as an orderly in a nursing home in Milwaukee, I was found to have an aptitude for medicine. One of my specialties as a medic in high demand was providing proctology services.

You did not misread that. *Proctology*—the branch of medicine concerned with the anus and the rectum. I don't know what kind of person dreams of that as their future. Not me. It was *not* my fantasy. Trust me. Yet my reputation soared. Some of it was basic: lancing boils, treating hemorrhoids, and so on. Some of it was more complicated. We'll leave it at that.

Admirals, captains, commanders, and lieutenants, all the top brass, would only allow me to work on them. The line I later used (but chose not to repeat to Brooke, for the time being) was that I was practicing my skills for Wall Street, by becoming an expert in dealing with assholes. Like I said, proctology was never on my dream radar.

Maybe one of my ancestors had dreamt of becoming a doctor and had passed that along to me in their DNA. It was my interest in, commitment to detail, and process, AND "dexterous hands" that caught the attention of a young US Navy cardiac surgeon, who became a mentor to me and gave me the opportunity to work for him at the Veterans Administration hospital at Fort Miley, San Francisco. (Remember the hands part, because this resulted in a lesson that comes under the heading of "transferable skills.")

A feeling of euphoria marked my arrival in the Bay Area. At last my dreams of expanding my horizons—literally—were coming true. There was nothing like the first glimpse of the Golden Gate Bridge, which comes into view once you climb to the top of certain San Francisco hills. Everything that had ever been sung or said about the city had not been made up in the least. In those early days of acclimating, I used to imagine the reactions of ancestors who had migrated westward, like some of the first Pony Express drivers who happened to be Black. Most had chosen their daunting job for the opportunity to make some money, probably never planning to relocate. But I'm guessing that when they arrived—as far west as you could go—and caught their first sight of the Pacific Ocean and miles and miles of uncultivated fertile land plus all the business potential for shipping by water and rail, their plans to return to wherever they had started their journey might well have changed. And new dreams were begun.

There I was, beginning my dream of going to medical school and joining my mentor as a heart surgeon. Life was grand. This was my oyster, and I was there to discover my pearls. Unexpectedly, after a couple of years, my new dream took a surprising turn when my girlfriend, pursuing her degree as a dentist, became pregnant.

By this point in my life, I had been married once, only briefly, and was in no rush to head back down the aisle. But now the time had come to keep the promise I'd made to myself as a little boy. There was no way, as a medical student for God knew how many more years, I could support a wife and child in San Francisco, one of the most expensive cities in the world. And the medical field was changing, not necessarily for the better. Trying to make it in the field without a child was hard enough. For a while, I stuck it out at the VA, adding new sources of income by doing some house painting, demolition and renovation work, and lawn mowing.

When Christopher was born, he instantly proved to be the most astounding human being on the planet, my soul child. He was the best dream come true I'd ever known and the son I'd promised all my life to be there for—no matter what. He gave me a renewed permission to dream, as if daring me to get out of my comfort zone and dream bigger.

So, soon after becoming a father, I gave up my surgical scrubs and traded them in for a shirt and tie, merging my interest in medicine with a job selling medical equipment and supplies. The top producer in my group was a hotshot clearing $80,000 a year. Not bad. My goal was to be as good as him, if not better.

Then along came the red Ferrari. The driver, to whom I will be forever grateful, not only took me onto a trading floor for the first time but answered my questions *What do you do?* and *How do you do it?* in detail, and he was forthcoming enough to say that he was clearing about $80,000 a month. This was a no-brainer. Why would I not pursue an opportunity to earn twelve times as much as I was hoping to earn selling medical equipment by doing something that had captured my imagination?

Chris Jr., at this point, was about four months old. His mom and I were already having problems, but when I announced my plan to eventually secure a job in the arena of Wall Street—first by landing a spot in one of the trainee programs available at a handful of brokerages—she flipped out. The tension between us brewed for months. The internships were few and far between. Doors weren't exactly *slammed* in my face, but nobody was interested in a Navy veteran without even a bachelor's degree.

Was it racism too? My answer is that it was place-ism—as in, I did not come from a place that would connect me to money. True, I did not come from a wealthy or political family. And, no, I had never gone to college. The issue was: "Who's going to do business with you?" Place-ism, as I explained it to my granddaughter, can affect anyone.

But I wasn't worried. This was my dream, and from the moment I'd felt the energy, I knew the financial services business was where I was supposed to be. All I had to do was land an internship and I'd be on my way. Brooke was curious why I didn't give up but hung in there—especially with all of the challenges, rejections, and place-ism.

One reason: my mother had told me, "Son, you can do or be anything."

Brooke couldn't hold back. "You believed her!"

Those words were the Gospel. "You can do or be anything," I repeated. Those words had become my mantra for life.

The other thing I'd learned to say to myself was "Nobody can stop you but you." No matter how many doors were slammed or gently closed in my face, I wasn't quitting. Nobody could stop me but me.

Then, all at once, a few life-altering events took place. First, I received an offer from a brokerage to start their program in two weeks. *Yes!* With great pleasure I gave notice at my sales job and decided to start studying ahead of time. Big mistake. On the day I was supposed to start the program, I arrived early only to find out the guy who had hired me had been fired. *No!*

This was a crash course in not banking on anything until the check has cleared. Worse, I will tell you that unemployment can put a real damper on your love life. Naturally, I hustled up painting jobs and yard work and whatever I could do to bring in money. But for my soon-to-be ex-girlfriend, the mother of my son, it was too little too late. My dreams were never going to amount to anything, in her view. When I insisted that I wasn't giving up, she was unmoved. At an impasse, we argued heatedly, and she called the cops—who discovered that I had a serious backlog of unpaid parking tickets. Over a thousand dollars' worth. Money I did not have.

Originally the police took me to the downtown Berkeley jail to be held. Since all this had gone down on a Friday, guess what? No court until Monday morning. When I finally walked into court, I was informed that the rule in California was explicit: if you can't pay, then you've got to stay.

Before I could ask any questions or send out for legal help, I was shipped off to Santa Rita County Jail for ten days. That was my sentence.

We're talking about *parking tickets*. The name was a lie. It was not a jail. It was *prison*. One of the largest prisons in the United States. Not *any* prison. I found myself at the very same time in the very same prison that held the most notorious prisoner in California—who had chopped twenty-three people to death with an *ax*! TEN DAYS! (Let me pass along some free unsolicited advice. If you've got any unpaid parking tickets outstanding, put this book down right now and go pay your tickets.)

The hardest part of the ordeal—which, by the way, included being sent to solitary confinement for mouthing off to a guard—was that this was the first time I'd ever been away from my son even for a day. For the prior fifteen months, Chris and I had at least seen each other first thing every morning and last thing every night. As the days passed brutally and slowly, all I could wonder was *Does Chris Jr. know that I didn't leave him, like my father left me?*

The question ate at me for those ten days, and I had no means of calling and checking. To complicate everything, on the same day that I was transported back to the Berkeley jail to await my hearing with the judge, I was supposed to have a job interview.

"You're not going to believe it," I recalled to Brooke, "but it was the end of the line, the last office on my list. All my leads had run out. This was the last chance for me to get into a trainee program." In the holding cell, I asked to place a call to Mr. Costello, who was supposed to interview me. The guard who let me make the call had no idea how much he would have a hand in changing the course of my history. Mr. Costello was fine about postponing our meeting until very early the next morning.

Finally, after seeing the judge, who cleared my record after time served—wiping clean what I owed of the twelve hundred dollars in fines, fees, and penalties—I raced back to the place that we used to call home, a knot of dread in the pit of my stomach.

Somehow I KNEW. Fear pulsed in my blood.

You ever know something in your gut, and no one has to tell you? A quick glance through the window at our house confirmed my fears. They were gone. My ex and my baby son. Vanished without a trace. The car was no more. The place was emptied of every piece of furniture, every kitchen pot and pan, every stitch of clothing. This woman took everything but the DUST!

Imagine if the one dream, the one decision, the one most important promise you've been determined to keep, has suddenly been smashed to bits in front of you. For all I knew, my ex would try to spite me and keep Chris from me forever. That was my level of panic and despair. Everything that mattered had been turned upside down and inside out.

These moments were too raw to share with Brooke, though I did give her some of the broad strokes. At least this way she would understand how much my most urgent, most ferocious dream of being reunited with Chris Jr. had managed to save me.

The next fifteen hours after my arrival home were a blur, but I do remember getting a few hours of sleep at a friend's place—where I washed the same clothes I had been wearing when the officer hauled me in for parking tickets.

At 6:15 the following morning, I made it to the interview with Mr. Costello.

Hearing this, Brooke braced for disappointment. That was kind of how I felt when the man who greeted me at the firm did so by giving me a brief once-over and saying, "Deliveries in the rear."

Taking the proverbial bull by the horns, not even pausing to think, I responded, "Mr. Costello, today's probably the most important day of my business career and I must admit that I'm underdressed for the occasion."

"Well," he replied, "you've got that right. What happened?" With that, the two of us sat down in the office's waiting area as I fumbled for an answer.

For the life of me, I couldn't think of a lie bizarre enough, so I told the truth. It was the best thing I could've done.

Brooke squinted her eyes at me, like *How could that be?*

As I proceeded to tell the story to her, all these years later I could still see Mr. Costello sitting there and listening to me with a stony face until he finally spoke and said he could relate.

"How?" Brooke asked.

"Turns out this guy who interviewed me had been married and divorced THREE times!" The more I thought about it, the less I decided to go into detail with Brooke. But, mannnnnn, he told me some STUFF with those stories!

After twenty minutes, he looked me in the eye and said, "Be here Monday and I'll personally walk you into the trading room."

You never know how powerfully the truth can shift a conversation.

This was more than my dream. It was an open door to opportunity, a first step on a long climb—but a step even so. In my imagination I could picture an ancestor, somewhere, far back in my history, who dreamt of a future in the field of finance but who never walked through the door. Now I had.

For the next couple of months, my ex called occasionally to let me hear Chris Jr. in the background. It was cruel and unusual punishment. Some days I thought it would break me, but I had to stay strong to fight to get my son back. Ask any parent who has been separated from his or her child, and you will hear about the anguish and the torture of feeling powerless to change it. All you have is the dream of being reunited.

To keep it together, I threw myself into my training program and studying for my licensing exam as a matter of life or death. As the lowest intern on the totem pole, I was given phone lists to call that were probably invented to discourage the most motivated trainee. Other guys who, like me, still had to pass the licensing exam at least were given qualified leads and even business that was already set up and just needed paperwork. What I lacked in opportunity, I decided to make up for by working harder and more efficiently than anyone else. My *very* dexterous hands became cold-calling machines. I could dial any phone number on the telephone with one finger, and I kept another ready to click off the call so as not to have to hang up the receiver. Instead of hearing rejection, as soon as I detected that someone wasn't interested, I thanked them and went to the next call. It was jazz. Before long, both of my index fingers had become permanently bent. Plus, I started to sell. Whoa. All of a sudden, more senior brokers wanted me to be on their teams. Before, they'd looked at me, a Black guy without a college degree (unlike the other African American in the office, who'd gone to Stanford), and weren't interested. Now they were.

For the time being, I politely told them that I'd go it on my own. In the short run, that was dumb; but over time, my choice not to hitch my wagon to somebody else's was smart. All the newer brokers warned me that I'd have to take the test a few times. Though I said nothing, in my head the mere possibility was unacceptable. There was no room for failure. I had to pass the first time. And, in fact, I did, advancing to the yearlong training program at the firm with the princely monthly stipend of a thousand dollars. A little over half what I had been making selling medical equipment. It was enough for me to get by if I kept rent low—six hundred dollars a month at the Oakland rooming house where I was staying. The grind was actually a godsend, keeping my mind off the pain of being separated from my son.

Finally, after a period that felt as if it had gone on forever, at about one in the morning one night, there was a knock on my boarding room door. When I opened it, right there in front of me were my ex and Christopher.

My ex said very little, other than basically telling me, "Here, I can't do this anymore," before she took off, leaving my son with me.

In a state of overwhelming relief, I hugged him tight, only then realizing what had just happened. The boarding house didn't allow children. None of the places I could afford—where you pay for a room, a hotplate, and maybe share a bathroom—would allow kids, especially a toddler.

So just like that, Chris Jr. and I became homeless.

* * *

Brooke had already heard snippets of some of these stories about when her dad was little, but as we continued to walk and distract ourselves to stay warm, she wanted to know every detail.

"Winter was hard," I confessed. "Not cold like this, but there were some bad storms, and I was pushing your dad, a growing, hungry baby boy, in a stroller up steep San Francisco streets. Everything we owned was in the stroller or on my back—a big thing of Pampers, a briefcase, clothes and toiletries in a couple of garment bags that I had slung over my shoulder."

"But where did you sleep?" she asked, wanting me to just lay it all out.

"Well, we slept sometimes on BART. That's the train system. I'd pick him up from day care and we'd go ride the train to the end of the line. We'd go in the last car where no one could see us. He'd sleep and I'd study books on investment and high finance, and read from the latest economic journals on market trends. Sometimes I'd get us a motel. If we were lucky we'd stay at Glide Memorial Church's hotel. That was the first hotel in the country for people who didn't have homes of their own. You'd have to get in line early or there would be no rooms left, and you'd have to leave early with all your stuff. But it was clean and safe, and they had showers."

Brooke made the comment that Glide Memorial Church must have been like an Underground Railroad.

"Oh, you don't even know the half of it. They had a soup kitchen. With all my favorite soul food. Your daddy ate so much of that food, I think that's how he got so huge."

Brooke had made the connection. We had been given shelter at Glide and on BART as stops along the way on our own

Underground Railroad. We had been given a reprieve from the storm and had used our power of dreaming to keep from becoming too discouraged. Just as I was about to add that we also slept on the bus, finally I heard the sputter of an engine and saw a snow-covered Chicago bus approaching. We were half a block away from the bus stop.

To make sure that the bus driver didn't miss us, I leapt into the street and started waving like a madman. The bus stopped, mercifully, and the door folded open.

Relieved and grateful, I followed Brooke up the steps and into the toasty warmth of the bus. The driver didn't look old enough to drive a car, let alone a bus, but he was in charge. When I took out my twenty, he shook his head and proceeded to tell me that they didn't take cash for fares. We needed a prepaid bus pass or ticket.

Needless to say, I didn't have anything resembling a pass or a ticket.

Brooke gave me a look that said it all: *Poppa is out of his element.* She leaned in and whispered, "You don't ride the bus, do you?"

"Not in a long time," I admitted.

News alert: everything's automated. You get an electronic ticket pass at a kiosk or metro station for the bus and the train. I remember in the good old days buying a ticket on one bus, and if needed, they'd give you a transfer for another. If you were going north-south, you could get a transfer to go east-west.

In San Francisco and then later in New York City, I was once king of public transportation. Clearly no longer.

The young bus driver must have taken pity on me. He motioned us to the back, saying, "Have a seat."

Brooke found a row away from the other passengers and slid

in next to the window. In San Francisco, I told her, buses were our main Underground Railroad. Chris Jr. and I used to live on the bus. We slept, ate, and changed diapers on the bus.

"This didn't make me too popular with other passengers. At night, when the BART train wasn't running and the buses had stopped, sometimes we slept in the BART station bathroom in Oakland. We played a game so he wouldn't be too noisy. We pretended to be invisible. If somebody knocked on the door and yelled, we couldn't say a word. The game was called Shhh."

Brooke and I held our fingers up to our mouths, both saying, "Shhhhh," at the same time. "Was he good? Did he fuss too much?" she asked, concerned.

"No, he was perfect. He knew that we were going to the Promised Land and this was our dream. He would get real quiet and would fall asleep in my arms."

Brooke and I got quiet too, and we checked out the scenery outside the windows. I exhaled heavily.

"I'm going to remember what you said," Brooke reflected. "You can *do* or *be anything*."

"It's true." I shrugged.

Then, as a note to herself, she quietly added, "And nobody can stop you but you."

FOUR

THE POWER
OF ONE

Brooke and I were silent for some minutes, watching the frozen urban scenery pass by, almost like an old black-and-white movie—in slow motion. We were still up Beyond the Wall in a rougher, bleak part of town, but the unplowed snowdrifts—piles of pristine ice and snow everywhere—made everything look serene, almost beautiful. Mercifully, the bus's heating vent right above our heads sent down a continual stream of warm air that made us feel like we were in the tropics compared to where we had just been.

It wasn't until we spotted a couple of teenagers walking briskly past the bus that I realized we were moving at a snail's pace. Maybe I muttered something about the underage driver who'd apparently never driven a bus in a snow siege, or quite possibly it was just my loud internal monologue. In any case, Brooke read my agitation and decided to distract me with more questions.

For starters: "Poppa, why do some people give up on their dreams?"

"You know, there are a lot of reasons for that. But if you want me to give you the main reason, I think it's because they never learned about the Power of One."

Brooke glanced around the bus at the five or six other passengers on our slow boat to downtown Chicago and leaned in, asking in a whisper, "What's the Power of One?"

I paused, wondering where to begin. At that moment I happened to look out the window again and saw something that offered a most usable launchpad.

"You know what that is?" I asked her, pointing to a lone shopping cart, far away from wherever it had originated and now left out on the sidewalk to withstand the storm.

"That?" She squinted her eyes at me. This had to be a trick question. "It's a, whatcha callit, a grocery basket. Right?"

She was right, I assured her. "But for anybody who's ever had to be on the run, it could be a car or even a mobile home."

Brooke, still dubious, waited for me to explain.

* * *

Anyone who has ever heard me speak can attest to me making a few key points. In so many different ways, I was taught, *No matter how ambitious your dream, don't ever let anyone tell you that you can't do that. If you want something, go get it. Period.* This applies not only to something you want to make happen for yourself but also to solving old problems or improving life in your community and in the world.

What I had to figure out on my own—through much pain and perspiration—was that trying to turn a dream into reality meant that I had to lead the way. Nobody was going to be there calling out directions for the best way forward. This was on me. If I fell or took a wrong turn, nobody was sitting around waiting for my call asking for help. Maybe my initial assumption that it was otherwise came from watching old movies on TV with Moms, who loved the toughness of Bette Davis and the he-men of the old-fashioned western movies. Sometimes it may seem so, but life isn't a movie. No matter how arduous the journey, even when I found myself in dire circumstances that I frankly did not create, I had to learn there were no bad guys to blame, and there were no good guys riding in to the rescue. You can look up at the horizon only so many times or listen for a stampede of horses coming your way only so many times. The truth is—*The Cavalry Ain't Comin'!*

Not only is the cavalry *not* coming but also that cloud of dust, that thunder causing the ground to shake, the pounding of hooves you hear in the distance, that MIGHT be a posse! Meaning—things may be about to get WORSE!

This is always tough for me to explain because I believe that angels in human form will show up at our low points to encourage us. But we can't pin our dreams on anyone but ourselves. No matter how parched we are, crawling all alone across the desert to our goals, with no water in sight and a target on our backs from incoming fire, we do not have permission to fall down and curl up into a ball and cry until help arrives. We cannot slip into a hole of despair or fear, because that is quicksand.

We have to become our own cavalry. Each of us, individually, has to demand of ourselves: *What can I do? How can I, on my own, turn my dream into reality? How can I see a wrong and try to make it better? How can I out-dream this trouble?*

That's a simple explanation of the Power of One.

Once you accept responsibility to dream a better way forward for yourself, the smallest of actions you take can have huge consequences. There's another phrase I use that's probably been translated into more than forty languages, including most recently into Arabic, and it reminds us of the power I'm talking about: *Baby steps count to, two, too, 2, II.*

Whether you've heard it from me or someone else, it's understood the world over to mean that in pursuit of the Universal Dream (our very own American export), personal or collective transformation may not conclude overnight or within weeks or months. Yet the minute it starts as a dream, you have begun. You have changed your mind and your life. And as long as you keep going forward, those baby steps will turn into leaps and bounds, and eventually into hurdles, catapults, and ultimately into flight.

Ask the Wright Brothers. Ask Elon Musk. How many times were they mocked and told to call it quits? How many times did they have to return to the drawing board?

Ask Rosa Parks. Her first small step in helping propel the Civil Rights Movement and take on the monster of segregation and white supremacy was to take no step at all, a choice NOT to budge when she was told to go to the back of the bus. She was tired! She sat down and refused to be moved. She was the cavalry and a catalyst. That's the Power of One that unleashed the Momentum of Many.

During this same year when my granddaughter and I were on our expedition Beyond the Wall into the desolate cold of Chicago, a fifteen-year-old Swedish teenager named Greta Thunberg took her first steps toward becoming one of the world's foremost voices on climate change. She didn't want to be singled out as a hero or heard because of her stark words; she wanted to sound multiple alarms about doomsday scenarios becoming real, scenarios backed by science. Her first public action was to persuade Sweden's parliament to pass laws for the country to swiftly become carbon neutral.

When later she was patronized by world leaders who insisted they were making hopeful strides, Greta famously responded, "I don't want your hope. . . . I want you to panic. I want you to feel the fear I feel every day, and then I want you to act. . . . I want you to act as if the house was on fire. Because it is."

Greta has galvanized a global movement of young activists who are inheriting a planet that may not be inhabitable for many more generations. To them it's personal. Without concerted action, there will be no future for them. All of the people who have joined the dream of saving Planet Earth have added their own individual Power of One to what has become and must continue to be an unstoppable effort on the climate crisis.

In explaining this concept to Brooke, I had to admit that for most people to care about a shared dream, whatever the issue happens to be, it's human nature to ask, "Well, what does this have to do with me? And can I really make a difference?" Once they have a connection, or know someone, or have the problem in their own backyard, or are directly affected by the issue, that's the Power of One. They have just added themselves to the equation.

Economic gyrations and vast social inequalities have only worsened with the turbulence of climate change and mounting global health calamities—all having an impact on the essentials of water, food, and even air. When natural resources are imperiled, so too is civilization. With massive spikes in global homelessness, there is no doubt that the map is changing. It's been estimated for some years that approximately 2 percent of the entire population of human beings on the planet are on the run. Women, men, and children are running from war, gender violence, ethnic and religious conflict, and revolution in the Middle East. They're running from ethnic and civil wars and extreme climate change in sub-Saharan and Western Africa. They're running from gangs, drugs, violence, and political instability in Central and South America. Whole communities in impoverished coastal areas are running from extremes in weather and the destruction of entire ecosystems. Wherever they're from, they're running for similar reasons—toward more ample resources, toward freedom, opportunity, employment, all for their very lives and the lives of their loved ones. Some have found temporary shelter in refugee camps, but overcrowding and other adverse conditions in those settings have made their stays increasingly tenuous. Some run to places that once gave them refuge but have now shut their gates. Some are caught in the middle, locked out from where they came and from where they're headed.

I once saw a broad estimate that said if all of these adults and children, homeless and on the run, lived in one place at one time they would instantly become the tenth largest country in the world—with a population greater than Russia, Mexico, or Japan. Unless you understand what it is to be on the run, you might refer to them—like much of the Western press does, American media in particular—as migrants, immigrants, refugees, even infiltrators (as I've heard them called in my own country, sadly).

Brooke asked what I would call people from other countries who are fleeing poverty and persecution, and I gave her my view that we're all members of the same family called humanity. So that would make them my kin. "What else do I call them? I call them survivors."

My mother, Brooke's great-grandmother, was no different from many moms around the world trying to flee domestic violence— many of whom have to grab their children and everything they can carry and flee for their lives, in some cases traveling unbelievably long distances. Some even have to travel with their kids and all their worldly belongings in shopping baskets like the one we'd just seen left out in the snow.

"One night when I was seven years old," I recalled, "Moms hurried me and Ophelia outside, where we saw most of our things piled into one of those grocery carts." My mother had tried to leave previously, but my stepfather had come home before she could get us out of there. This time she had planned for the right moment and had secured a new place for us about four blocks away.

We must have moved well over a dozen times. Interestingly enough, every move somehow took place within the same four-block square of real estate in the inner city of Milwaukee. No wonder I couldn't wait to travel to other places.

I also learned very young how important it was to memorize the exact street name and number where we lived. To this day, every address where we ever lived will be forever imprinted on my memory because of how often I watched Freddy come close to killing my mother, and each time I'd have to run to the nearest pay phone to call the police, begging them to come to that particular address.

The other thing I learned young, like anyone on the run, was the importance of having a key to the next address where we hoped to live.

That night, after Moms made it clear that we had to move quickly, we took off. Timing was critical. Freddy had gone hunting that weekend, but he could change his mind and return at any minute, as he had before. Any hint of where we had gone, he'd find us—which meant that the beating Moms would get from him would be that much worse. We moved like a SWAT team, all of us clinging to the shopping cart and rolling it as fast as we could to the new place. It was a modest two-story flat with a big broad tree out in front. With the moon shining through the branches, it looked like something you'd see in a storybook. Just as we stood there, catching our breath, I turned to see my mom digging furiously through her purse and searching her pockets. Somehow, in our haste to leave, she had left something important behind.

With tears in her eyes, my mother shook her head and told us, "I forgot the key. I must have left it in the dresser. We can't go back. It's too late. He could be home by now."

For one minute it was like our dream had been shattered into a million pieces. But then, stubbornly, I guess, I pointed up at the tree and vowed, "I can get us in."

My mom and sister looked at me skeptically.

"I can," I insisted. "I can climb the tree, scoot out on the branch, drop down on the porch up there, climb through the window, and then come downstairs and open the door."

Brooke, spellbound by this recollection, worriedly leaned in. I was about to describe my mother's disbelief when my granddaughter shook my arm and begged me to cut to the end. "Did you do it?"

"You bet I did. I climbed that tree like it was nothing. Slithered out onto a branch and dropped onto the porch. The tricky part was climbing through the window. Luckily, it wasn't locked! As I crept through the flat and down the steps, it was *darrrrkkkk*, but this was our dream, and I wasn't giving up. Not on me and not on my mom and sister."

There are some joys you can give to the people you love that have nothing to do with money or material things. That was it for my mother. When I opened the door to let her and Ophelia in, along with our shopping basket, my mother's face was so happy and relieved I wanted to freeze it like that and always see her in my memory as I saw her in that moment just before she hugged me tight.

That is the Power of One. When you think there's absolutely no way you can make it and you're about to give up on your dream, it takes just one person—you—to make a difference.

"Years went by before I was ready to tell anyone about being homeless," I confessed to Brooke.

My granddaughter nodded thoughtfully as if she completely understood. Speaking very softly, she asked, "Did anyone at your job ever find out, you know, that you didn't have a home or a car or anything? Did you talk to anyone?"

"Let me start with the second part of your question. I talked to Chris Jr. nonstop from the minute I picked him up from day care to the minute he went to sleep. He was a great listener. And he talked up a storm too."

It had always been my baggage: my concern about people seeing us and knowing our situation. It's strange how on the one hand you can feel so horribly invisible to the rest of the world that seems to be doing just fine, but on the other hand you become self-conscious that someone will see you and know your story. The only place where we could be visible was at Glide. Everybody who sought refuge there had their own stories. Everybody there who was trying to change their situation understood the Power of One. Nobody sat in judgment.

It surprised me how none of my coworkers ever seemed to figure out my other life.

"No clue?"

"Everybody did know I had a son. Maybe they figured there wasn't a mom in the picture. But what they didn't know was that after I picked him up from day care, I'd come back, do more work, and sometimes the two of us would sleep under my desk." The only person who might have been suspicious was one of the partners, who loved to come in at the crack of dawn. He used to give me a sideways look when he'd see me up and at it, with little Chris at my side, dressed and ready to go to day care.

At the office, whenever we had lunches for clients or special conferences—with pizzas and sandwiches—I'd be right there, wrapping up the leftovers. My coworkers joked all the time, "Man, that Gardner can *eat.*" Little did they know that there were two Gardners who could really *eat.*

At a certain point in our journey, to be able to eat and afford day care, as well as to save up for a place to live, I started to donate blood to supplement our income. The blood banks paid in twenties, and I had a self-imposed rule to avoid breaking a twenty. In my mind, if you had to spend four dollars on milk and cereal, once you broke the twenty it was going to get spent fast. At work, commissions had begun to trickle in, but I put that money into the bank for housing and refused to touch it, until about a year after I'd become a single, homeless father, when I was ready to start looking for our first home off the streets.

* * *

The last time we'd actually lived at an address we had resided in Oakland. When I finally found somewhere for us to live, much to my surprise, my search had taken us full circle—to a little house in Oakland. I had looked everywhere in San Francisco but had returned to the East Bay for a place I could actually afford. How many times I had passed it but never noticed the place, I couldn't tell you. We might have missed it altogether had it not been for a sign from heaven that drew me toward it: a rosebush in bloom, right there in the ghetto.

Little Chris and I had survived three seasons without a home—fall, winter, and spring—and as the heat in the East Bay began to set in for summer, I wasn't sure we could tolerate another three

months. My concern about spending the money was not having
it in the event there was a downturn in the market—always a
possibility—and then we'd have to go back to living without a roof
over our heads.

"You were worried?" my granddaughter asked.

"Of course. But it hit me one day that it was time to stop worrying about what could go wrong because it was keeping me from
dreaming about what could go right."

Brooke wanted to know how long it took to find the place
with the roses in the ghetto.

"About a month."

The timing was perfect. There was no FOR RENT sign, and the
place looked like it needed some cleaning up and a little TLC.
When I spotted an older gentleman working outside the house
next to it, I asked if he happened to know the owner. He did know
the owner because, of course, he *was* the owner.

That was another good sign. When I asked if he'd be interested in renting the place, he said he would, adding though that it
would have to be the right tenant.

Telling him that I was interested, I asked if there was paperwork to fill out. The kindly, older gentleman didn't need to do
a background check or anything. He had seen me with Little
Chris, and after I told him that I was a single dad just getting on
my feet as a stockbroker, he stopped me, saying, "That's all I need
to know. When would you like to move in?"

"You know," I recalled to Brooke, "when I picked up the key
and went to get Chris from day care, I felt like someone had written a million-dollar check to me and it was in my pocket. You
should have seen the look on his face when I put the key in the

door and we walked into our own place. There was a big bedroom your dad got to have all to himself."

"You made it to the Promised Land." Brooke had followed all of the lessons I had been sprinkling over our conversation like manna, about how dreaming can take you from your hardest days to your *one day*s.

In the morning after our first night in the new place, when the time came to get ready to go to day care, Little Chris became concerned that we hadn't packed up all of our stuff in the stroller.

"You know, Brooke, that's how cycles can become generational. My son—your father—had seen me carry everything that we owned, every day, everywhere for almost a *year*, and it had become normal for him."

Imagine, I asked her, what he was thinking as we prepared to leave and I was NOT carrying anything. Chris Jr. pointed at my garment bag and at his little pile of clothes and said, in alarm, "Poppa, you forgot this. And this . . ." And then he added, "We have to bring our stuff."

I can't explain what it felt like, at long last, to be able to say, "No, son, we don't have to carry anything anymore, because we've got a *key* now. We're *home!*"

He looked at me uncertainly. At that point I held out the key and showed him again. "See, this is our key. We're coming back tonight. We can leave our stuff and it's all gonna be here when we get back."

Little Chris was so concerned that I had to let him put the key in the door himself and see that it really worked.

Brooke couldn't help but laugh. Neither could I. The other

people on the bus seemed slightly annoyed that we could laugh so hard in the middle of such gloomy weather.

"The funniest thing of all was the sight of Little Chris in the stroller. By this point he was so big he couldn't fit anymore, and that was when we upgraded to a bigger vehicle."

"A grocery cart?" Oh, Brooke was *on* it.

"Yep." We were a famous sight in Oakland and Berkeley, all right. We went everywhere in that shopping cart.

With those words, I suddenly remembered how money got tight at one point, as I had feared it might, and, to my horror, we arrived back at our new home in Oakland one night only to find out that PG&E couldn't wait another day to get the nineteen US dollars that I owed them and they'd turned the electricity off.

After a year of the most intense struggle conceivable, I didn't know whether I was going to QUIT, CRACK, or CRY! Instead of doing any one of those things, I took a baby step hopefully in the direction of normalcy by deciding to go ahead and give Chris Jr. a bath by candlelight.

When in doubt, *adapt*, I told myself. But as I got my little boy into the bath and began to wash him, I remember asking myself doubting questions for the first time. These were questions I had avoided all this time like—*How much longer can I do this? Where am I trying to get us to? What's going to happen next?*

My son picked up on my energy, stood up in the bath tub, looked me straight in the eye in the candlelight and said, "Poppa, you know what?" Before I could respond he followed up with, "You're a GOOD POPPA!"

Now if that doesn't get your fire going your wood must be WET!

We were going to be okay. And on a side note, I will mention that PG&E later went into bankruptcy. After all, karma apparently has GPS.

Dreams—if we are willing to let them unfold and take us on their ride—may require us to accept that the way forward will be one of nonlinear progressions. Rarely do we have the option to move along from A to B to C. But no matter how much uncertainty and hardship comes our way, we have to be mindful of the smallest blessings that can ignite the *biggest* fires in us all.

If we stay true to the dream, progress does reveal itself.

Glancing out the window, I was grateful to see progress revealed. It appeared that, at least for the moment, the precipitation had stopped. The sky was still gray and foreboding, but much to my relief we were getting close to where we'd first veered off North Michigan Avenue. We had returned from Beyond the Wall, back to familiar sights that I actually hadn't thought about in years.

* * *

Before I had a chance to point out an important personal landmark—the YMCA where I had sent the kids when I was first building my business in Chicago and very much on a tight budget—I noticed in the distance what was left of the housing project known as Cabrini-Green. I directed Brooke's attention toward it.

"What's Cabrini-Green?" she asked, trying to see where I was pointing.

Even though some of the institutional brick units still stood behind fencing and there was a nearby row of newer low-rise units, in the snow and ice, the mostly abandoned project looked like a frozen graveyard for buildings. The main residential towers, once conceived to house low-income residents in modern comfort, had been torn down. The whole expanse, stuck in the middle of pricier real estate, reminded me of a graveyard for well-intentioned efforts that went awry.

"Cabrini-Green," I explained, "became one of the most dangerous places to live in Chicago. It was crowded and poor, and had terrible problems with a lot of drugs and gangs."

Without using the words, we discussed the issues of white flight and gentrification and, yet again, how easily families can slip through the cracks and become homeless.

Fifteen thousand residents had at one time been packed into those towers and lived there in that small park-size stretch of land. Eventually it turned into a war zone. The news told of kids getting killed in the crossfire between rival gangs. Children and adults suddenly disappeared. When sociologists went in to try to evaluate how Cabrini-Green had become one of the most notorious and violent housing projects in Chicago, one of their conclusions was that the units had been built to house families with mothers and fathers as dual heads of households. In actuality, the overwhelming majority of inhabitants had been teens and young single mothers—very few adult males.

One dedicated community activist had exemplified the Power of One when he attempted, as an adult male, to mentor many of the younger men of Cabrini-Green. Suddenly there were fewer criminal arrests, improvement in school attendance, and more lawful employment. But when that leader had to leave to pursue his dream of running for political office, there was no substitute for the hands-on work he had been doing. No one stepped in to take his place.

It wasn't that leaders and citizens didn't care, I told Brooke. From my now wiser and older perspective, I guessed the decision to tear down Cabrini-Green had to do with economics. Real estate developers had no doubt been eying the property for a long time. City Hall went along with them. Private investment built up the surrounding neighborhoods with businesses and pricier housing, but nobody could figure out what to do with the few folks left in the project.

"All that potential," I couldn't help saying to Brooke. "All those young people who could have been given the permission to dream but never were." The city struggled for years afterward to come up with solutions because obviously the problems of drugs, gangs, poverty, and a lack of better options don't just vanish when you tear down buildings.

Brooke turned her head back to catch one last look at Cabrini-Green. "What happened to all those people? Where did they all go?"

"We don't know. We should. When they tore down the towers, all over the United States different cities were also tearing down 250,000 units in housing projects. That's basically a million people. Gone."

We were both at a loss for words.

There is no easy answer or one-size-fits-all solution to homelessness—whether local or global. Yet I had to feel that if we didn't learn urgent lessons from past failures, the cycle was going to continue.

During our silence, I had a series of stark observations about what happens to individuals as well as to groups of people who have been denied the permission to dream. Clearly, it's not enough to have good public policies designed to help people achieve better lives when those folks aren't empowered to be part of the solution. When you can't see a thriving future for yourself all you know is how to keep living the way you've been living—even when it's intolerable. It's a collective Groundhog Day. It's just as the Dramatics sang in their 1972 hit, "Whatcha See Is Whatcha Get." Your external circumstances are impossible to change when you lack the capacity to imagine possibilities that may not be right in front of you—*yet*.

The consequences of not being able to develop that capacity can be dire. In my case, of course, that capacity was nurtured by a mother who told me that if I wanted to be world-class at something and become a millionaire too, I could do that and be that. That doesn't mean she did the dreaming for me. That's where this idea of *permission* comes in. When you help someone else *choose to believe* in themselves and their most audacious, wildest dreams, you are also giving them permission to be different. And also to be criticized, scorned, and mocked.

My thoughts took me back to high school and to a lot of my peers who never gave themselves the permission to verbalize or visualize another existence outside of poverty or struggle. The person who came to mind was this one kid who was apparently threatened by anyone else's dreams and differences. He made it his job to bust anyone with lofty goals. He was like the Sheriff of Lower Expectations. We've all known guys like him. Usually they are the loudest, most arrogant, and most intent on putting others down to compensate for their own lack of anything remarkable. They are the same guys that never try, never grow, never change, never dream. Inside they probably wish they could break out of their own limitations but you'd never know that. You think something might happen to jolt them into revising their thinking and sometimes it does. Not with this kid. Forty some years later, he was still the same—still the loudest, most arrogant, and most stuck in the same situation as he was in his late teens and early twenties.

Actually, I'd run into him at some point in late 2017 when I happened to be in Milwaukee to receive a community award. Whenever I thought of him, I'd remember the time back in high school when I made the mistake of sharing my latest dream of becoming world-class at something with him and how arrogantly he had responded.

First thing he did was LAUGH.

"Laugh all you want," I replied. "You'll be hearing about me. I'm gonna do big things. And I'm gonna be a millionaire."

He went off on me. "What do you mean . . . *a millionaire*?" Before I could respond, he blasted me with his bull-horn of a voice, taunting, "How you gonna be a damn millionaire. You can't sing. You can't run and jump and catch a ball. You ain't that good looking and you ain't gonna do no big things. And you sho' ain't gonna never be no millionaire."

Well, as I didn't have to remind Brooke, nobody else was going to change my choice to give myself permission to dream. He did, however, make me think twice about sharing my plans and visions so readily.

As the years went by and my travels took me far away from Milwaukee, I had no idea what had happened to him. That was, until this recent visit home when I was invited to test drive a particularly flashy car that the dealer hoped I'd consider purchasing. It's a heady feeling when you go to take a look at the latest model Rolls Royce with all the bells and whistles and the salesman tosses you the keys, telling you, "Take her out for a spin."

A magnificent car with dark tinted windows, it made me feel like James Bond. Not necessarily a fit for me, though the Rolls was a vivid symbol of how far from your most humble beginnings your dreams can take you. For some reason I decided to drive through the old neighborhood and cruise past some of the old spots where my friends and I used to hang out. That's how I caught up with the same person who said I was never going to achieve anything for all the reasons that he listed.

At first, I couldn't believe my eyes. Up ahead of me on the left, he was standing out in front of one of those same spots where a group of us used to gather without much else to do. Now he was in a group of older guys who were like a cautionary tale for what happens when you don't give yourself permission to dream. They all looked like him, as if frozen in time, only grayer, more overweight, more cantankerous and curmudgeonly. Hidden behind the tinted glass, I approached him slowly.

As I described this encounter to Brooke, she blurted out, "Oh, no you didn't!"

"I couldn't help it." With a tap of a button, I rolled the window down and nodded my greeting.

Brooke asked breathlessly, "What did he say?"

"I can't repeat it," I admitted. "But I think he realized that maybe he should have spent more time dreaming than trying to stifle someone else's dreams."

My granddaughter nodded in agreement but I could see a

question bubbling up inside of her. With a gentle, "Hmmm?" I prodded her to ask away.

"I was just wondering how the Power of One could help people who didn't get taught they could do or be anything."

An excellent question. "One way is to be an example," I offered. That's why I had decided to create an internship program once I'd gotten my business rolling in Chicago. We employed inner-city youth who came in part-time and learned about the world of Wall Street and high finance, and, if they kept their grades up, my firm paid for their college education. One of our interns who went on to attain her undergrad degree and her masters in finance later recalled how this experience changed the way she saw her own potential.

The more I thought about it, the more it seemed that the time had come to expand that approach, perhaps to dream a more urgent dream. The time had come to get others to see their own possibilities for making a difference. The time had come to rock the boat a little, not to mention the vote—to get others to care more about issues they think can never touch them or their families, and to add themselves to the equation.

Realizing that we were not far from another important personal landmark, I suggested to Brooke, "How 'bout we jump off at the next stop and stretch our legs?"

With a nod, she checked to make sure her harmonica was still snug in its case inside the plastic bag that was tucked under her coat for extra safekeeping. Then she rose from her seat and followed me back up to the front of the bus.

FIVE

CHANGE THE GAME

In a near miracle, as we disembarked the bus we both noticed that the wind coming off the lake was oddly still. No longer pelted by snow and rain, we were happy to be out in the elements, at least for the time being. Our pace picked up, not in desperation to escape the blizzard but in exhilaration that we had apparently survived it.

"Let me see if I got this right," she started off. "If someone has a dream to get rich one day, let's just say, all you need is the dream and not to give up on it. Is that all?"

I promised to get back to her on the merits of a dream of being rich, if that's a person's sole dream, but I did remark, as my mother once did to me, "There's a whole lot of people who have money, but they ain't got the honey." In other words, people who pursue riches alone may well attain them, but they often find their lives lacking in meaning, purpose, and love. The honey is what makes dreams so sweet that they can feed and sustain us over the long haul. The honey enriches your entire life, not just your bank account.

"But," I went on, "to your question, the first step to turning any dream into a reality is to give yourself permission to own it. Except that's the easy part." The hard part, I reminded her, was that if you want to make your dream a reality and more than a wish, "you gotta have a PLAN."

Brooke shook her head, as though I'd been holding out on her all along. As a challenge, she countered, "Did you always have a plan?"

"Nope, not really. Not until my dream evolved and I decided to move to Chicago and change the game—to build my own company at the same time that I suddenly became a single father of not one but two kids."

Brooke looked at me in amazement. Somehow she had never heard the saga that my son and my daughter have lovingly called *The Pursuit of Happyness: The Sequel.*

"Ever heard the saying that lightning never strikes twice?" I asked my granddaughter.

She had heard it before.

"Well, I've got a story to tell you that will prove that saying wrong."

* * *

Plans, like dreams, have to be adaptable, enough so that you can allow them to evolve as your circumstances change and your vision grows. I'd spent a year of my life trying to gain a small foothold at the first stockbrokerage that opened its doors to me, and honestly, I hadn't fleshed out my plans much beyond continuing to climb there.

Once I settled Little Chris and myself into our new home and began to master the fundamentals required to try to build what was known as a book of business—the evidence started to show in the activity of, and indeed the creation of, new accounts. Not only did I have a solid grasp of the overall financial services business, but also within this sphere I had begun to shine.

The more I understood the business, the more my dream to become world-class pushed me to seek out the Jedi masters of my field. As my good fortune would have it, New York–based Bear Stearns had just expanded from mainly being a brokerage house to a full-service investment firm. It was a new world. In their San Francisco office, headed by Marshall Geller and Gary Shemano, the door was open to anyone the partners deemed to have the ultimate degree: a PSD—Poor, Smart, and with a deep Desire to become wealthy. The objective of those with a PSD was to ultimately acquire an MBA—a Massive Bank Account. Recounting all this for Brooke, I could see with hindsight that the challenges of the past had turned into advantages for my future.

With my signing bonus from Bear Stearns, I was able to move us into a beautiful apartment in San Francisco, which cut down on the daily three hours of commute time. Located on the pan-handle of Golden Gate Park, our new address was close to Chris's day care and the expense was no longer the issue it had been. I also was able to expand my wardrobe from two suits (one blue, one gray which I'd been wearing every day for a year, and which I'd humorously called my Civil War reenactment uniforms) to include two *new* suits. And you guessed it: one blue, one gray—but this time we're talking Armani power suits. (Hey, it was the '80s!)

Whenever I heard from my ex, I couldn't ignore a hard-to-resist passion that I felt for her—despite all we'd been through. The chemistry was *powerful* even if we were completely incompatible as far as making a life together. Once we'd split and she'd left as she had, there should have been no way that I even considered any kind of reconciliation.

That being said, on the occasion when she came to visit and see our son, I was in a very different place. All the things that she had said would never happen were unfolding, and I was not just being mentored by some of the best in the financial services field; I was positioning myself to transfer to the mothership: Bear Stearns in New York City. Say what you will, but the Best of the Best in many fields—finance, fashion, art, entertainment—all "made their bones" in New York. As the Sinatra song says, "If I can make it there, I'll make it *anywhere*!" My plan was to master my craft by learning from and competing with the Best of the Best!

My reunion with my ex was joyful. Chris Jr. loved having his parents in the same place. Caught up in my ex's charm, I wanted to believe that the past was behind us, that we had become wiser and could maybe even create a new life together if we could only build on the success I'd achieved and our mutual adoration of our son.

In that spirit, my ex and I agreed to get together later that night to talk about reconciliation. One night. We should have *talked* more! By morning, we both realized reconciliation would *not* work. What did work was the blessing who arrived nine months later when we became parents of a beautiful, strong-willed little girl, baby Jacintha—J., as we called her.

That's what I mean about lightning striking twice. We were not supposed to be together long-term, but those romantic fireworks were real, striking at two different times in our lives. We were clearly meant to bring those two souls into this world. Brooke may not have quite understood how unlikely the odds were for conceiving a child on that one reunion night together, but she did grasp the fact that Little Chris and J. would grow up with a powerful sister-brother bond.

My ex and I agreed to share custody of our son and daughter. The plan was that they would stay with their mom during the school year and with me during the summers and over holidays. They were in Los Angeles most of the time, which wasn't the worst place to visit, and truly, it would have been tough having them year-round once I made the big move to New York City to work under none other than the legendary Alan "Ace" Greenberg, chairman, CEO, and senior partner at Bear Stearns.

Warren Buffett once said of Ace, who happened notably to be a member of the Society of American Magicians, "Ace Greenberg does almost everything better than I do: bridge, magic tricks, dog training, arbitrage—all of the important things in life."

Brooke was intrigued. "Magic tricks?" she asked.

"Ace was known to be one of the best amateur magicians around. He was world-class, and I got to learn from him." His example, I told Brooke, helped me to realize that you should never be afraid of your own magic.

Sometimes your magic may lead you to discover your own way of doing things that doesn't necessarily comply with how everybody else does them. But before you break rules and change the game, you have to learn the rules.

On my very first day at Bear Stearns in New York, Ace gave me two pieces of advice that I've carried with me every day since: "Get smart quick," which for me meant continuing to learn the business from the *best* in the business. And "Invest your time before you invest your money."

My plan began to crystalize gradually. An eye-opening realization came from the discovery that there were rock stars out there doing a totally different type of business from what I was doing, and they were making *real* money—meaning annualized rollover money. They were making exponentially more than those of us doing transactional trades. They were, in effect, managing and investing money for high-wealth individuals and farming out work to brokers. Their growth model and their earning capacity were enhanced by new relationships, which were coming through the pipeline constantly.

In a retail brokerage, where I was, you merely do transactions—make a sale, make another sale, and pursue the next sale—without creating a stream of relationships and revenue. Before long, I started to feel the sizzle of a radical idea. Instead of the money manager farming out work for me to make the trade, why couldn't I fulfill both roles? Why couldn't I do that for accounts that ranged from high-wealth individuals to institutional clients to middle-income folks who weren't getting financial guidance for increasing their wealth? Once I began to understand the institutional investment management business, being a retail stockbroker was of no interest to me. I had seen the future.

Meanwhile, even though I was earning an improved income in New York, Ace's other advice about investing time rather than money early on went somewhat unheeded. This was the 1980s, after all, and it was New York City, where everyone was rapidly making boatloads of money and spending all of it just as fast.

None of that overly concerned me because I thought I had discovered what was going to allow me to be Miles Davis in my own right and change the game. Besides, I'd found a market that was not being served or solicited, a market that frankly no one on Wall Street had ever acknowledged existed. This market was "small" (valued at less than one billion dollars), and it happened to be owned and controlled by African American business people and entrepreneurs. Going after that market, however, would mean bucking the Bear Stearns mothership, which determined what investment packages and financial products we were to sell. Towing the company line became harder for me.

When I tried to go after my own opportunities, the hierarchy at Bear Stearns attempted to rein me in. Ace Greenberg admired my ambition, but my immediate superiors weren't happy and wanted to fire me. Though Ace was in my corner, ultimately his hands were tied.

In a soul-searching moment, I had to adapt my plan. Later, those moments came to be known as instances when you have to "pivot." Sometimes, as I like to say, you are forced to make a "hard pivot." It might be something you would have never chosen but you have to make it work. My hard pivot was going to take me in an unexpected direction.

Brooke appeared to follow the general details of my decision-making with clear understanding. She made the interesting observation that soul-searching was a lot like dreaming and trying to get an answer from your dream.

She nailed it. My soul-searching soon delivered the answer: Chicago. It made all the sense in the world.

At the time, Chicago and the Midwest were Timbuktu. On the one hand, even though it was a hop, skip, and a short airplane ride to New York, Chicago was like being on a different continent. On the other hand, the region was home to the one of the highest concentrations of tremendously successful African American entrepreneurs who had created true generational wealth, iconic brands, and enduring businesses. I'm talking John H. Johnson of Johnson Publishing, Ed and Bettiann Gardner of Soft Sheen, and of course Detroit's Berry Gordy of Motown.

As someone who was raised in the Civil Rights Movement of the '60s and '70s, and as someone who had marched for freedom and equality, I believed that laws alone weren't enough to protect our rights as Black citizens; what was needed as well was *economic* equality achieved in real terms—as business owners, as board members of global corporations, and as investors with the power to control capital and amass true wealth. Part of my dream was to play a role in facilitating that empowerment. I also had a crazy idea that the pensions and savings of individual working-class folk of all backgrounds—union members, teachers, nurses, firefighters, city workers, and so on—could be making them more money if invested collectively.

All along in my journey on Wall Street I had become more and more convinced that a lot of folks who weren't at the highest economic levels were missing out on opportunities to achieve real wealth—simply because they didn't have access to the best expertise.

All of that pointed me to the Windy City.

* * *

By the time I made the move to Chicago in late 1986, almost all the money I'd earned had been spent, leaving me to arrive with only a hundred dollars, a dream, and a plan. I'd come full circle—from the Midwest to the West Coast to the East Coast and back to the Midwest. Some people have learning curves. Others, like me, have learning circles. The Midwest had taught me in my youth to dream of doing something bigger than what I saw every day. The West Coast was where I'd obtained the opportunity to enter the world of the dream, and the East Coast had been about mastering the skill set. Back in the Midwest, it was time to *get to work*.

At the age of thirty-three, coming full circle also meant that I was only ninety minutes from Milwaukee, Wisconsin. Moms could come visit me, and Chicago was a great town for the kids to come stay with me during the summers and for the holidays. Thanks to one of my mentors, whose exceptional generosity and belief in my dream eventually led to a start-up grant of ten thousand dollars, I put stakes down on a small apartment where I lived and worked, and quickly learned the lay of yet another city and a new cast of characters in the investment world. I would later dub this "building my Rolodex" (remember that old-fashioned phrase?) because relationships are more important than money. They are infinitely more valuable than what you've got to sell.

For a full year, I kept my nose to the grindstone, earning my membership on the Chicago Board Options Exchange and the Midwest Stock Exchange, as well as my NASD membership, and getting my broker-dealer registration. Every day, every week for a year. This required total and complete focus to the *n*th degree. Before I ultimately began to build the business that would be the first of its kind in Chicago, I had to establish myself, hang out my shingle, and learn something very important: I had to learn what I did not want to do! The lesson arrived, at long last, on a Monday morning in October 1987, when I officially opened up shop.

"Everything was great!" I told Brooke, hinting only that something was about to throw a wrench into the works.

She waited for the plot twist.

"Well, the same morning that I had chosen to be my first day in business was October 19, 1987, what soon became known as Black Monday—the *worst* drop in the Dow Jones Industrial Average in a single day. *Everrrrrrrr!* Worse than the drop in 1929 that kicked off the Great Depression. Worse than the one-day drop in October 2008 that wiped out whole sectors of the global economy."

"Oh no!"

Oh yes. The stock market lost 23 percent of its value in one day—which has never been topped since. Everyone took a hit, especially the little guys like me at the time. The lesson learned was I did not want to live like that. So I immediately made a *hard pivot* to focus on the institutionalized brokerage business. Changing the game was now on a fast track.

This was by no means an easy environment in which to launch any financial services company. However, guess what? My previous experience with homelessness became an asset. You may ask how. It's simple: when you're homeless, you're basically working with *no* resources—so you become *very* resourceful.

Brooke had heard the word "resourceful" before but had to admit she never had really understood it. We discussed resources that weren't about money—things like ingenuity, initiative, resilience, and a refusal to give in even when calamities occur, like the whole stock market crashing.

"Attitude is everything," I emphasized. "If I had to live on oatmeal for a year, I could do that." Brooke, who loves oatmeal, thought that was a no-brainer.

You have to draw from every lesson learned—from your own experiences and from those of others. Then there's what was later called "Guerilla Marketing," by which you create your own playbook and make things happen on the fly that nobody else is doing. Though I didn't invent it, I certainly mastered the 101 version of it.

"The way I see resourcefulness," I suggested, "is that you use what you have until you get what you *need*." Entrepreneurs and game changers generally have to be resourceful, often finding opportunity in the midst of adversity. Something like 50 percent of Fortune 500 corporations were actually founded during either a bear market or a recession.

What many entrepreneurs discover is that you don't really *pursue* a dream as much as you *build* or *make* it. Sometimes you have to do all of those things at once. That's Guerilla Marketing 102. Pursuing my first institutional client for a solid year was all-encompassing, though for the most part without too much stress. So much of building my dream was laying the groundwork—creating, cultivating, developing, and nurturing new relationships. Things were really moving along even if I had yet to lock down the business. But I wasn't worried. That is, until the following fall and winter when the weather started to get cold and I hit a cash-flow snag—which can happen—and my phone got turned off!

Now I was in *trouble*. After trying to go it alone and compete with the biggest names on Wall Street for a portion of the billions of dollars in commissions that were paid out every year, and after developing all those new relationships, suddenly I had no telephone?

This was a nightmare scenario.

Q: How do you work as a stockbroker without a telephone?
A: You DON'T!

Back then you couldn't work without a fax either, another piece of technology needing phone lines that many of Brooke's age rarely comprehend. That too was cut off. The phone company had no compassion.

All the potential new clients had just heard from me that I would take care of them if they gave me their money . . . *except that, oh, um, I was not able to pay my phone bill.* This was bad, and if people found out, it would be disastrous.

"What did you do, Poppa?"

Well, in those moments you have to think like Ace Greenberg and use every magic card you got up your sleeve. I got *resourceful*!

Some of the worst days of winter hit that year (not unlike the blizzard weather that Brooke and I were in the midst of encountering). Forced to make a hard pivot, I had come up with a risky plan. Instead of sitting by the phone that wasn't going to ring, I went out into the freezing cold and made the rounds to everyone on my latest contact list—without an appointment. These were executives and decision makers at the offices of all my potential clients—pension funds, unions for firefighters, cops, and teachers, *everybody*. They saw me and waved me on in—probably because they were so surprised I would come out in such adverse conditions.

The meetings all ended with potential clients saying, "Good seeing you, Chris. Call me next week." Meaning they had no reason to call me and learn that my phone service had been disconnected.

The move gave me enough time to collect the forty dollars or so that I needed to pay to have my phone service turned back on. And I probably got three times as much business out of it than if I hadn't gone out.

"Back in—" I stopped myself from referring to "the olden days." Instead of telling Brooke that I had turned lemons into lemonade (way too old and corny), I went even older, offering, "To quote William Shakespeare, 'All's well that ends well.'"

Brooke, satisfied with lessons on the power of dreams to change the game, apparently noticed that I had slowed to a standstill in front of a large residential building at 555 West Madison. "This is the Presidential Towers," I announced.

She looked it over with approval. It had been impressive, for sure, when I moved into it as my second Chicago address. The rent was a few notches above what I could easily handle but the apartment was much improved at doubling as a residence and an office. Some days I got caught up in the glamour of being an aspiring entrepreneur on my way up, but mostly I was simply another American Dreamer—trying to open the doors and keep the proverbial lights on. When things were tight, I'd often head home from meetings and come around the corner hoping not to see my furniture piled up out on the street. I never knew. But there were other surprises.

"One morning," I began, "I walked out of the elevator and into the lobby here at the Presidential Towers and I saw this beautiful little boy and thought, *That little boy looks just like my son.*" I then described how that little boy jumped up into my arms, exclaiming, "Poppa!" It *was* my son! And just past him was my daughter, Jacintha, and their mom . . . and all of their luggage.

Stunned and not at all sure what was happening, I guided everyone into the elevator and up to my apartment-office. As soon as they filed in behind me, I immediately stepped into the wash-room to throw some cold water on my face—literally—and when I came out my EX was gone.

Again!

Yep, for the second time lightning had struck. That's what I mean by my having a sequel to *The Pursuit of Happyness*. In these episodes, I had advanced from struggling to opening up my own firm and barely avoiding getting evicted on a daily basis to now being a single father of not one but *two* children.

"See what I mean? You need a plan that covers the things you just can't plan on."

Brooke nodded as if all the pieces of the puzzle were finally fitting together. Her next question caught me off guard, though. "Did having them with you give you more meaning, purpose, and love?"

It did, I assured Brooke. They were what gave my dream its honey. "Except of course when they acted like normal kids who do dumb stuff."

Earlier I had shown Brooke where her dad and aunt used to go to the YMCA's summer camp and also their day care center. Now I told her about one time when Chris and J. were about eight and four respectively. They used to ride the bus home together, and I'd wait for its arrival in the afternoon, then meet them as they got off, and then we'd come back to the apartment together, where I'd work some more. But one day Chris Jr., in charge of their bus fare, had spent all the cash on snacks for the two of them. So they had no money for the bus.

"On snacks?" Brooke asked.

"They had a packed lunch but decided to get chips and candy or whatever else they could get that they preferred." Without money for the bus, they had no option but to walk all the way home. No small deal.

Brooke and I continued over to the place where the bus used to arrive, and I showed her where I was standing when the bus stopped and they didn't get off. The driver said he hadn't seen them. Terror gripped me that something unspeakable had happened. My greatest fear was that if they had missed the bus and had no choice but to wait for the next bus or walk, Chris Jr. might have thought it was easier and faster to take a shortcut through Cabrini-Green.

Brooke, having heard earlier about the notorious housing project where kids had gotten shot and had disappeared, could only say, "Oh no!"

For the next hour and a half, I divided my time between running up and down the streets they might be walking down and dashing back to check other buses. Finally, I saw the two of them strolling down Halsted Street—Chris Jr. holding J.'s little hand.

Before I really let him have it, I listened to Chris tell me what had happened, and he admitted to his poor decision to spend their bus money on junk food.

The fact that he took responsibility was encouraging. And I had to cut him some slack when he was quick to add that he knew better than to take his little sister through Cabrini-Green. So they had taken the long way home. After that, I couldn't be too mad. Both he and J. promised never to spend bus money on snacks again. Some lessons you only have to learn once.

Brooke and I had been given a reprieve from the weather, but I could feel a new stirring of wind and snow. The warning was there: time to head home. But there was one more landmark I wanted to share with her. There were also a few more important lessons to pass on.

Magically, just as these thoughts occurred to me, a taxicab appeared almost out of thin air right alongside us at the curb.

SIX

A BLUEPRINT FOR YOUR LIFE

Chicago architecture, in my humble opinion, is some of the most impressive, eclectic, and beautiful in the world. As our taxi maneuvered its way south, I directed Brooke's attention to some of the city's iconic buildings, telling her anecdotes about the architectural history that fascinates me.

"You know, in a couple of the Batman movies, the directors chose to use sites in Chicago to represent Gotham City—even though the DC Comics creators based it on New York." That led me to telling her about how even though this city was the birth-place of the world's first skyscraper, Chicago was always being overshadowed by the Big Apple. "You know, that's why they call it the Second City."

She hadn't seen the Batman movies in question but was eager to know what landmarks to look out for. Our cabdriver was *into* this discussion. He said he'd be happy to show us a couple of the spots. Why not? For starters, scenes from Wayne Enterprises were shot at 330 North Wabash—which looked even more stark on this snowy day, all gleaming and modern. Built in 1971, it was the last building designed by the iconic modern architect Mies van der Rohe, whose minimalist black glass tower was the epitome of world-class design and helped give *The Dark Knight* its timeless feeling.

The cabdriver thought there was a big old chase scene in *The Dark Knight*, with the Batmobile driving underground and then morphing into the Batcycle, all of it shot speeding down Wacker Drive—the only Chicago street that has a North, South, East, and West. There is also Upper Wacker, Lower Wacker, and Lower Lower Wacker, corresponding to its multiple levels. I always used to say, "Hey, if you want to have a meeting with someone and hope they don't show up, tell 'em, 'Meet me on Wacker.'" Works every time.

"My favorite building is at 35 East Wacker," I admitted as the cab sped off in that direction. When its highest stories came into view, I told Brooke, "It's called the Jewelers' Building, and as you can see it's a jewel." At forty stories high, it was built in the 1920s, and it was where the jewelry exchange used to be.

The architectural style, known as neoclassical, emphasized centuries-old elements with both grandeur and simplicity— giving the building a feeling of wealth and value, perfect for what jewelry merchants and other prominent lessees would want. All exclusive.

From what I had heard, the building had a car elevator, and in the days of Al Capone, if he was running from the law, he could just drive into the building, go up the elevator, drive out onto the upper floor and have a meeting, then get back into his car, come down the elevator, and drive off. Nobody ever knew.

Before we proceeded to our next stop, Brooke asked if we could circle the block and give her one last look. She was mesmerized. In fact, she seemed to have remembered a trailer for a Batman movie that had a building like that in it.

"When I fell in love with architecture," I commented, as we set off again, "I was a few years older than you, about fourteen years old. Dr. King said something about architecture in a 1967 speech, and it changed how I saw myself and how I saw my future. From then on, I could never look at a building the same way." The speech was about the importance of having a blueprint—for your success, for your life, and even for a movement to create social change. A blueprint is more than a plan; it's a foundation—a cornerstone.

Brooke had heard me talk about the Civil Rights Movement but had never heard how I became involved as a teen activist.

"Well, first of all, in the 1960s, every young African American person in Milwaukee was conscious of the movement." Organizers were on the move—like Dr. King's Southern Christian Leadership Conference (SCLC) and the National Association for the Advancement of Colored People (NAACP), among others that ranged from nonviolent to militant. Activists mobilized in every part of the country, drawing attention to long-standing systemic racism. Much of what you heard on the news was about injustice in the South. Yet it was everywhere.

Milwaukee, then and even later, was harshly segregated. As a little boy, I'd convinced myself that everyone in the world was Black. Except for on TV. Brooke couldn't understand how it was possible to never see a white person for eight years. "Remember I told you no matter how many times we moved, we stayed in this same four-block square? African Americans could only rent in certain areas." We were so stratified the city was basically divided between north and south. If you were Black, you had to stay on the North Side, except for the fact that most of the factories and foundries were on the South Side. Every morning there would be a large migration of workers of color trekking over all three bridges, and that wasn't a problem. But once the sun went down, no African American wanted to be caught on the wrong side of any of those bridges.

Brooke followed my words with alarm and disbelief.

This was an important conversation, and I didn't want to sugarcoat it. "You know that Dr. King himself was surprised when he came up to Chicago for the first time and found out how segregated it was—even worse than Alabama!"

In Milwaukee, the big focus for organizers was a push for open housing legislation. Starting in August 1967 we marched for two hundred nights. Ultimately, the March on Milwaukee would be seen as one of the movement's most successful marches at effecting real change on the local, state, and national level. This included the passage of the federally enacted 1968 Fair Housing Act.

My friends and I were in our early and mid teens, and none of us had a clue about what "open housing" really meant, but I was excited to be in the movement. The NAACP Youth Council, under the leadership of Father James Groppi, was based at Saint Boniface Church, across the street from our then-home.

We marched, we made fliers and posters, we protested, we had organizing meetings, and we had somewhere safe and social to go after school. "But the best part," I confessed to Brooke, "was that after we marched, they *fed* us!"

Next thing I knew, I had to break out singing our anthem song, Billy Paul's "Am I Black Enough for You?," chanting, "Freedom, hallelujah, lead 'em . . . My kids could dig it more if I *feed 'em*!"

The organizers were smart enough to know that you never let a good crisis go to waste. I was over the moon just getting out of the house, but add sandwiches and cookies to the deal and I'd march all day every day. We protested in the rain, sleet, and snow, out on the streets like the US MAIL.

We were also empowered at a critical time in history. Besides the Civil Rights Movement, there was a cultural, musical revolution taking place, a peace movement kicking up in response to the Vietnam War, and then the women's liberation movement on top of that. Between Miles Davis and Dr. Martin Luther King Jr., I had two very different but lasting influences.

Moms approved up to a point. She worried a little that I might get too militant. When I later brought home a copy of H. Rap Brown's "Die N——r Die!" my mother made it clear, "No, uh-uh, you can't be up in here with all that now."

Another time, when we all started buying clothes at the

Army-Navy surplus store, I got a big Army-green khaki jacket and a black-and-white checked scarf that unintentionally made me look a little like Yasser Arafat.

Moms took one look at me and said, "Hmmm, and what facet of the PLO do you represent?"

She really didn't mince words.

When our NAACP Youth Council started selling sweatshirts—complete with sayings on the back like SOCK IT TO ME and BLACK POWER and SOUL SISTER or SOUL BROTHER—I got my mother one. She wore the sweatshirt with pride, although she was not out in the streets marching. Moms had grown up in Louisiana and had been denied her teaching credentials because of her color, and she understood the struggle. My opinion is that her oppressor had been her abusive husband, and the effort to survive his violence took up all the fight she had in her.

One day, however, I caught Moms in a show of activism. At the time she was wearing her sweatshirt and sweeping up the kitchen when all of a sudden an oversize cockroach appeared.

"Ewwwww," Brooke responded appropriately.

Moms turned to me with a smile and said, "There go a soul brother right there—look at him." All of a sudden my mother became absolutely militant, wielding her broom and cracking that cockroach in his tracks. *BOOOOOMMMM!*

Then she was quick to add, "Sock it to me, Black Power!" And she broke out into the biggest, most beautiful laugh. Moms didn't laugh much. It was, I know now, part of the pain of dealing with an oppressive relationship. Though when she *did* laugh, it was contagious.

Moms and I actually didn't talk much about the marches and

the speeches I heard, but of course the assassinations in those years—first President Kennedy in 1963, then Dr. King in April of 1968, and Bobby Kennedy in August of 1968—were like we had lost members of our own family. Especially Dr. King. For some strange reason I can remember that when the news came on the radio, they played Sam Cooke singing "A Change Is Gonna Come." In my saddest moments of loss, I can still hear his voice at the start of the verse . . . "I was born by the river . . ." and the sound of my mother's muffled weeping.

When I sang that line for Brooke, she softly asked which of Dr. King's speeches I meant when I mentioned my favorite. She guessed the "I Have a Dream" speech, given in 1963—his most-often quoted speech. After all, the subject we'd been discussing all day was the permission to dream. I loved that Brooke knew that speech, but that wasn't it.

Our cabdriver volunteered a guess that I had to be referring to the "Mountaintop Speech"—the last speech ever delivered by Dr. King. He had traveled to Memphis to speak that night in support of the city's African American striking sanitation workers and planned to lead a march downtown later in the week once he'd cleared the city's legal hurdles. It was the next evening, on one of the darkest days in world history, at around six p.m. on April 4, 1968, at the Memphis motel where he stayed regularly, that Dr. King was assassinated.

Our cabdriver had reason to mention what is an epic, unbelievable, prophetic speech. Every time I've heard or reread it, I agree with all who believe that Dr. King had foreseen what was to come. There had been death threats and a bomb threat on the plane he'd been on flying into Memphis. He even spoke of coming close to death years earlier when he was stabbed. He didn't know that he was delivering the last speech of his life that April 3rd, but he spoke as someone who wanted to make sure to say things he might never have another chance to put into words. Dr. King wanted to reassure and encourage all of us not to give up on the struggle, and to express his feeling that he had done his part, now it was up to us to keep going. Finally, Dr. King told us that he had been to the mountaintop and he had looked over to the Promised Land and had seen his dream of equality, freedom, and justice fully realized. "I may not get there with you," he said. "But I want you to know tonight, that we, as a people, will get to the Promised Land." He said he was happy and that he wasn't worried about anything and he had no fear of any man.

In recent years I've frequently been asked to deliver speeches of my own in recognition of the Reverend Dr. Martin Luther King Jr.'s birthday or for some special Black History Month/MLK Day event honoring him. Those are not easy for me to do because basically I quote him so often, from many of his speeches, and pay tribute to his leadership so regularly that every day for me is *his day*!

Still, when pressed to choose a special topic related to Dr. King, my go-to—my favorite—is perhaps one of his least known speeches and possibly the shortest he ever delivered. On October 26, 1967, Dr. King went to Philadelphia and spoke that afternoon at Barratt Junior High School—to students who were my age at the time. As part of a series of star-studded talks sponsored by the SCLC all across the United States, he had traveled to Philly to speak at a "Stars for Freedom" event that same night at the Spectrum—a newly opened, massive venue where he would be joined by the likes of Sidney Poitier, Harry Belafonte, and Aretha Franklin. What Dr. King and the most influential leaders of the Civil Rights Movement understood was that younger people were the key to true momentum for social change.

So, as I told Brooke, who was eager to find out why I loved this speech so much, Dr. King wanted to go speak at this local junior high school to invite the students to join their parents later at the Spectrum. This was brilliant salesmanship. He realized that if these kids went home all excited about attending the big event, their parents would want to get involved too. He wanted the students to recognize that they too had a role to play in the struggle for equality and justice. And then, instead of giving them, say, the young people's version of having a dream, he veered off in a direction I'd never heard.

With his usual oratorical simplicity and grandeur, he challenged the students to consider what would be involved in turning their dreams into a reality. In other words, what was their vision and the cornerstone of their plan? What steps would need to be taken? What materials and other ingredients would be required?

Dr. King began, "I want to ask you a question, and that is: What is your life's blueprint?" He didn't talk down to his audience, nor did he avoid complexity. Instead he followed a metaphor that encouraged everyone to think about the impressive buildings in Philadelphia and elsewhere. "Whenever a building is constructed," he went on, "you usually have an architect who draws a blueprint, and that blueprint serves as the pattern, as the guide . . . and a building is not well erected without a good, sound, and solid blueprint. Now each of you is in the process of building the structure of your lives, and the question is whether you have a proper, a solid, and a sound blueprint."

Dr. King reiterated the fact that every time you walk by any big beautiful building it might be easy to forget that *before* the dirt was dug, the foundation laid, and the building of it begun, early on it was only an idea, a dream, and then after that, a design made by an architect.

Brooke nodded with deep understanding. This was tangible advice she'd been waiting to hear. She could see that once you give yourself permission to dream, you are in charge. Nobody else comes in to do the work.

"That's exactly right," I agreed. "You become the architect of your dreams and of your own life—and the all-around contractor and builder."

To be all that, just like everything involved in the construction of a building, you have to have a "good, sound, and solid blueprint."

In this speech, "Your Life's Blueprint," Dr. King made it plain that as your dreams and plans evolve, hopefully your blueprint for a sound success will remain a guide throughout the building process. For it to do so, he believed your blueprint should contain three things: (1) a principle of *Somebodiness*, (2) the determination to achieve excellence, and (3) a commitment to the eternal principles of beauty, love, and justice.

A principle of Somebodiness, which Dr. King discussed as the first element in your life's blueprint, is

a deep belief in your own dignity, your own worth, and your own somebody-ness. Don't let anyone make you feel that you are nobody. Always feel that you count, always feel that you have worth, and always feel that your life has ultimate significance.

Brooke had said something earlier that day about the dream of being rich. I told her there was nothing wrong with aspiring to wealth and to the acquisition of financial security. In fact, I had come to the conclusion that the quest for prosperity and abundance is in our DNA—it's in our individual life's blueprint already. Your principle of Somebodiness tells you that you have what it takes to attain wealth, and you have the option to define it on your own terms, not the terms of others.

Yet your wealth and status, no matter how successful you are, should not give you your self-worth, in my opinion. "Your self-worth," I stressed to Brooke, "should never be equated with your net worth."

Brooke observed that my dream to become world-class at something was not so different from Dr. King's second item for a strong blueprint: *the determination to achieve excellence*, no matter what your field of endeavor. True. And I have always loved what he said to the students in Philadelphia and to all who got to hear a recording of the speech soon afterward:

You're going to be deciding as the days and the years unfold, what you will do in life—what your life's work will be. Once you discover what it will be, set out to do it, and to do it well . . . If it falls to your lot to be a street sweeper, sweep streets like Michelangelo painted pictures. Sweep streets like Beethoven composed music. Sweep streets like Leontyne Price sings before the Metropolitan Opera. Sweep streets like Shakespeare wrote poetry. Sweep streets so well that all the hosts of heaven and earth will have to pause and say, "Here lived a great street sweeper who swept his job well."

The first two elements important for every blueprint made sense to Brooke—and, by the way, our cabdriver seemed to enjoy the conversation immensely. But the third and most important element of all was harder to explain. What does it mean for a life's blueprint to have *a commitment to the eternal principles of beauty, love, and justice*? Simply put, if you are committed to these principles, the dream of the life you're building will be about more than just you. As Dr. King urged:

Don't allow anybody to pull you so low as to make you hate them. Don't allow anybody to cause you to lose your self-respect to the point that you do not struggle for justice. However young you are, you have a responsibility to seek to make your nation a better nation in which to live. You have a responsibility to seek to make life better for everybody. And so you must be involved in the struggle for freedom and justice.

He also put in a plug for being entrepreneurial and practical in service of the eternal principles, developing ways of solving problems with nonviolence or with militancy (as long as lives were not lost and property not damaged):

So our slogan must not be "Burn, baby, burn," it must be "Build, baby, build." "Organize, baby, organize." Yes, our slogan must be "Learn, baby, learn" so that we can "Earn, baby, earn."

In remembering so many of those lines, it struck me more intensely than ever that as a country we were still on the journey to the dream. We had a ways to go, but I had to walk the talk I always gave about "Baby steps count to, two, too, 2, II"—as long as we were going forward.

The "Your Life's Blueprint" speech changed my path, helping me appreciate the brilliance of the blueprints of some of the most iconic buildings in the world. Over time, after I finally had a running start to my business, I recognized the blueprint for my life and used it to expand my dream and fine-tune the plan for my business. An aspect to planning, I discovered, was continually raising my own bar. In naming my company, for example, I realized that if I wanted to compete with the top firms, I needed a name that sounded like a Bear Stearns or a Dean Witter. The most prominent names in the financial world, historically speaking, tended to be a conjunction of the two last names of the firm's founders.

That's how I came up with Gardner Rich & Company. It was that kind of name I could imagine not only on an office suite door but even on the storefront of an entire building. Most everyone assumed I had a cofounding partner by the name of Rich. Nah.

Brooke figured that one out as I recalled the story, though she was still curious how I came to pick that name.

"How could I lose with a name that made you feel you'd have folks tending your money like gardeners and enriching you and your investments? It worked. And you know what? You need to have a plan for tending and cultivating your dreams like a gardener so they really can enrich you."

"Did people ever ask where Mr. Rich was?"

"All the time!" I answered. "We just would say that he was in and out of the office."

Her laugh rang out in the back of the cab, and I laughed even harder. So did our friend behind the wheel.

Step by step, move by move, the day finally arrived when I was able to pick up the keys to my new office—in the same building that Brooke and I were fast approaching. Brooke had visited the place many times when she was younger, but it had been a while—over three years since I'd given up the lease.

"401 South Financial Place?" our driver asked as he navigated over slush and ice into the financial district, not far from the Sears Tower, onto the block where Gardner Rich & Company had occupied prime real estate for more than fourteen years.

As he pulled up to the curb, our driver thanked me a second time for raising Dr. King's emphasis on having a blueprint for your life and for sharing the need for a sense of Somebodiness. Assuring us that he would wait right there at the curb, he said, "Mr. Gardner, I wish that I'd heard a message like that when I was younger."

Something shifted in my brain as he said that. Like seeds being planted for a new thought. "You know," I began as Brooke and I stepped out of the cab, "talking to young people as a regular job might be fun."

She made me promise that the first school to get a visit from me would be hers. It was a deal. I'd get right on it. Were we serious? Was this a possibility? I would let the idea go and wait to see if it flew back.

We hurried over to peek in the windows of my former home away from home. This place had been magic. Memories came at me from all angles. My desk on the main floor had been a twelve-foot-long gleaming metal tail wing of a DC-10. Talk about a dream desk.

All around the office space we had displayed paintings and sculptures of African art and photos of my heroes, like Nelson Mandela and Dr. Maya Angelou and Quincy Jones, most of whom I had met and regarded as mentors. Two plaster elephant heads mounted on the wall had guarded the goods inside. Though I don't hunt, the elephant heads were reminders of my saying, "It takes as much energy to bag an elephant as it does a mouse."

We were all the lions, hunting the big game of opportunity.

Before being able to afford the lease, I had passed by this building on a daily basis for years and had pressed my nose up against the windows, dreaming of *one day*. In an era of cubicles, this was different—a big open office space (6,000 square feet!) on a single floor with an upstairs private area. Roughly 500,000 people a day walked past these windows. Talk about advertising! The dream came alive, and I thought about it all the time, continually creating real-world opportunities that would in turn give me the means to eventually afford to move in.

The winning feature was that it was right there on the ground level—making it easily accessible to any hungry applicant with a dream or looking for a proverbial foot in the door. That was my welcome mat. I'd not forgotten how discouraging it had been that I could never get an appointment with the CEO of one of the largest Black-owned businesses in the US. Every time I tried, I'd been required to go through one checkpoint and one gatekeeper after another on the way up to a penthouse suite.

An accessible operation represented more than my commitment to the eternal principles, as Dr. King urged us to have in our life's blueprint. Frankly, it was smart business. If I was being enriched by the soil of Chicago's wealthy and working folk, it made sense to help put resources back into that soil by hiring other PSDs like myself. And it paid off for all concerned.

"What made you the happiest?" Brooke asked before we turned to go back to the cab. "Buying the red Ferrari—or the Michael Jordan black Ferrari—or getting the keys to the office?"

Yes, getting those keys was a dream come true, and it was exciting to be king of the roost in that location and, hey, to own a couple of Ferraris. All of that was proof that with dreams and a blueprint, anything is possible. But again, those were just the trappings of success, I had to say to her, not the real source of a fulfilling life. Besides, Biggie knew what he was singing about in "Mo Money Mo Problems."

What was the real source of a fulfilling life?

Moments stood out for me: riding in a helicopter with Holly over a tropical jungle to a private getaway in Saint Lucia, pure heaven, pure peace; attending the graduation of my daughter, Jacintha, from Hampton University and watching her become the first member of our family to graduate from college since we came here in chains four hundred years ago; and hearing my son's news that he was going to be a dad and I was going to get to be a grandfather. To top all of that, I added, was getting to spend time with my granddaughter in a blizzard, and going Beyond the Wall and living to tell.

Brooke leaned in for a hug and reached up on her tiptoes to pat me on the back. We took a last look at the space my business used to occupy.

"So that's all I need to know—dreams, a plan of action, freedom to change the game, a life's blueprint, a belief that nobody can stop you but you, and when things look hard you can dream even harder?"

She hadn't missed much. That's the Honey Bear.

"Brooke, remember, your path may not always be in a direct line and you may not move as fast as you'd like, but it was Dr. King who said that the smallest actions, one foot in front of the other, lead to movement that creates change." To which I added my familiar refrain, "Every step counts, as long as you are going forward."

Brooke's face lit up, as if she had just recalled something lost long ago. It was a memory of the time when she was two and a half and I'd come to Boston to visit. I had taken her to a park not far from Harvard Square. Wow. I remembered it well—how she tried so intently to climb the ladder to the monkey bars, and like every protective grandparent, I had to stand right next to her, hovering and making sure she didn't fall.

Brooke repeated just what I'd told her. "Okay, baby, remember, one hand, then one foot. One hand, one foot." That was going up. That was how we were going to learn to climb that mountain. As the years passed, whenever she was learning something new, that was the drill: one hand, one foot. How was she going to master the harmonica? How was she going to become the star center on her basketball team? How was she going to get to the White House? Keep going forward. One hand, one foot.

That was exactly right, I assured her, and added, "Through the fire, through the pain. Baby steps in the rain. When all about you being the same, be the player not the game."

"Wow, whose quote is that?" Brooke asked.

I grinned. "Biggie?"

"Poppa, did you just *rap*?"

"Hey! You know how *we do*! We should call Jay Z and tell him that I'm ready to go into the studio!"

We laughed so hard at the concept, both of us, almost to the point of losing our footing.

A sudden blanket of new snow began to fall. The wind had picked up again, this time sharply. We had tempted fate by getting out of the cab. To our relief, our driver was still there, waiting for the next installment.

SEVEN

WORLD-CLASS SKILLS

When we jumped back into the cab, our driver had the engine running, the heat roaring, and the music piping. I listened for a couple of beats and recognized one of my favorite Stevie Wonder songs: "Rocket Love" from his *Hotter than July* album. The song took me back to those days after being homeless when Chris Jr. and I had just found our first place to live in Oakland. Our regular spot for a quick bite was this one greasy spoon—as they used to call them—where they let us eat on credit and pay at the end of the week when I cashed my paycheck.

Some days I was *so beat*, all I wanted to do was sit down, eat, and be still. But someone would always go over to the jukebox and put that song on. Immediately Christopher would jump out of his seat and look at me. "Poppa, it's Stevie! It's Stevie!" And we'd have to bounce to the chorus: "You took me riding in your rocket, gave me a star" and "dropped me back down to this cold, cold world" and I'd occasionally feel a little sorry for myself that my ex had bolted when she did and that it was still a struggle. But then the food would arrive, and I would watch my little boy eat with so much relish and joy, I could only feel grateful that we were making progress. One hand, one foot.

Genetics are funny. From a very early age Brooke shared a love for good eatin' with her dad. He relished food. That fact came up clearly at one point when I was in the middle of trying to get a handle on how my eight-year-old son was doing with his class-work. The question I asked him was "Son, what do you like best about school? What's your favorite subject?"

"Lunch," he answered, not even stopping to think.

When Brooke was about eight, I asked her the same question, and she did not miss a beat before answering, "Lunch."

Needless to say, once "Rocket Love" finished playing on the cab radio and I proposed that we grab a bite to eat somewhere before heading home, my granddaughter exhaled heavily. "I thought you'd never ask." She volunteered that she was thinking about pancakes and bacon at one of our favorite stops, the Oak Tree in the 900 Shops mall back up on North Michigan Avenue, next to the Four Seasons, which was an option for eating too, as well as the demarcation line that I referred to as the Wall. What the hell, we weren't going beyond it again. Or if we wanted to do that, we could.

"Let's see how we feel when we get there," I said.

On the drive there, slow and bumpy, with the sound of frozen partially plowed snow and ice crunching under our tires, there was a long enough lull in the conversation for Brooke to take out her Ferrari of a harmonica and play a few notes. Our cabdriver was almost too effusive in his compliments, saying he was amazed that this was the first time she had ever tried to play. Still, I had to agree. Brooke had a natural sense of pitch and her made-up melody sounded cool, and I told her so. Pleased, she tucked it away again, then put forward her next major line of questioning.

"How do you get to be world-class?" Brooke threw this to me like a test, as if we'd covered the steps in theory and now she wanted the practical lowdown.

"I am so glad you asked me that," I confessed. "The truth is that there are many masters of their trade who can't tell you how they got there. They just do it effortlessly. The only thing they all probably would say is that you have to be willing to grind in the early going. Learn the basics, improve, find mentors to challenge you, constantly ask questions, push yourself, and sacrifice. The harder you work, the more real your dream will become. But always remember to work more than you dream, never dream more than you work."

Brooke, somewhat disappointed, seemed to have heard all about hard work.

Then I went on to tell her how I had learned that lesson from Moms when she'd asked one day if I had finished my homework and my chores.

Moms: Son, did you do your work?
Me: Yes, Madame!
Moms: Did you pray on it?

Me: Yes, Madame!

Moms: Well, keep working 'cause God is *busy*!

Our driver muttered something under his breath, like *You know that*. Brooke had to give it up to her great-grandmother for telling me how it was.

My mother was so far ahead of her time. Along those lines, I'd talked to Brooke earlier about globalization and why the need to grind was so important. What many young people don't realize is that the competition for regular jobs is no longer from your peers but from overseas, where many of our industries have spent years relocating from our shores. That's why I have little patience when people complain about immigrants coming here to steal our jobs. Those who'd been coming and enriching our economy and culture for hundreds of years started here by doing the jobs nobody else wanted. Did an immigrant steal *your* job picking grapes? Washing dishes? Selling oranges on the freeway exit? Cleaning your windshield? Not at all. Corporations that offshore jobs to save money on labor and taxes, *they* eliminated your position. Companies that let employees go only a few years before their retirement, *they* are the thieves. Or the businesses that hire only part-time help so your pay flatlines while CEOs reap bonuses they don't need—that's who stole *your* job. Immigrants have nothing to do with that.

Some US industries that went offshore might never come back, it's true, but other kinds of businesses are ready to be reinvented and replanted here—with world-class leadership and vision, of course.

The irony, I pointed out to my fellow taxi inhabitants, is that, "Immigrants aren't coming here. They are staying where they are, grinding." With telecommuting and all the other ways companies can operate remotely, they don't have to come here to still compete for the same jobs. And the global competition for certain jobs—say, in the tech and customer-service arenas—was getting fiercer all the time.

"Are you with me?" I had to ask Brooke, who seemed to be following so far.

"Yeah, I think you're trying to say there's no room for half-steppin' right now. You gotta be world-class. Average ain't gonna cut it."

When your child or grandchild comes back with words you have passed on to them as if they are their own, that is a beautiful thing.

The choice to strive for excellence is all the more important now. "You have to make a choice as to whether you want to be the one signing the front of the check or the back of it."

Our driver, who had yet to volunteer his name, was more excited by that explanation than anything. "Man, that's dope, 'cause if you sign the front that means you the boss, if you sign the back, you just cashing the check."

Brooke probably appreciated the explanation but was intent on being given specific steps to become world-class.

"Fine," I said. "I have a few suggestions. But first and foremost, you'll need to do an inventory of your world-class skills, talents, and expertise."

Brooke approved of my summation of this first step. Ready for the details, she gave me her now familiar raised-eyebrow look of interest. "Go on," she said aloud.

* * *

Everything I learned about becoming world-class and developing the skills required for that pursuit began with my uncle Henry and his fishing tackle box. "What most people don't understand is that skills, like dreams, are transferable—"

"Excuse me," our driver politely interrupted. "Did you say *tackle* box?"

Brooke echoed his question. Neither one of them had ever learned to fish. Nonetheless, I proceeded to recall how Uncle Henry used to take me fishing and bring out a tackle box full of all kinds of stuff a world-class fisherman would want but might not need unless a particular situation arose. There was everything in there: specific kinds of lead weights, extra hooks and lines, different types of bobbers, a few lures, some sinkers, plastic worms, and cutters for removing a hook from the mouth of a fish still on the line, plus extra tools like needle-nose pliers and first-aid supplies.

Everything a fishing expert accumulates over a stellar career of catching fish usually gets stored in the tackle box. At some point you'll be glad that you were carrying around that special piece of gear you never used before. That's why an inventory can be helpful.

My best analogy was the Swiss Army knife. "You don't use all the different knives and files and clippers, but all of a sudden you have an emergency and nobody's got a bottle opener but you."

Brooke and our driver were now getting this down. So, they verified with me, did I mean that the tackle box is full of everything you've ever learned, and you may need certain expertise either a lot or rarely, but it's all in there?

"Right," I said. "You may have no idea at the time that the teacher who asked you to stand up and read out loud in class was preparing you for a career in sales or public speaking. You may have no idea at the time that the teacher who said you had an aptitude for math but weren't working at your full potential was preparing you to become world-class in the field of finance."

"That happened to you?"

"Oh yeah, in the eighth grade. She taught math and she was brutal."

At a time when my ultimate dream was to become Miles Davis, my math teacher flat-out said to me, "Chris Gardner, if you don't put effort into algebra, the only job you'll ever get in your life is driving the bus." Later in my career, I worked closely with organizations representing bus drivers, and many of them ascended to world-class stature as drivers and as leaders of unions and transportation agencies. That teacher should not have knocked bus drivers. Yet the way she said it to me was that bus driving was not going to get me to the places I wanted to go. She rubbed that into me and would even call me "Bus." I'd walk down the hall and she'd say, "Oh, here comes the Bus."

Her sarcasm worked because I did do well in algebra, and those higher-level math skills did get put to use in my Wall Street pursuits later on. Teachers do change lives—like Mrs. Mertz, my high school civics teacher, who made the rest of my life possible.

Brooke knew a little about civics from her plan to one day rise to the highest political office in the land. But neither she nor our driver were aware that there was a time in US public education when we were required to learn the fundamentals of civics—starting in grade school and then usually with a yearlong class in high school.

We were taught about the Constitution, about the three branches of government, about public service, and about the importance of voting and participating in our electoral process on the local, state, and national levels. We were taught that voting was a right *and* a responsibility. As young citizens, we were taught in school that we each had a role to play in civic matters. We were shown the connection between civic engagement and a strong economy. Mrs. Mertz emphasized that how we treated one another reflected back on us as individuals—making for a richer, more vibrant, cohesive community. We were also taught the values of equality, even if that hadn't been fully realized for all, and about the ideals of the American Dream.

Everything that I was taught about the promise of life, liberty, and the pursuit of happyness could be traced back to my civics classes. Maybe I didn't appreciate then how influential my teachers would be throughout my life, but I knew they were heroes. They instilled in me the basic principle that becoming world-class at something begins with developing world-class skills. Later, when opportunities arose that required me to push myself, those foundational lessons were in my tackle box. Not only that, but my appreciation for the work of educators helped me when I sought institutional clients, like teachers' unions and other educational organizations on the city, state, and national levels.

One of my first institutional clients was the Chicago Teachers' Pension Fund. Other cities' funds saw our track record and followed suit—across Illinois, Missouri, Kansas, and beyond. I was fortunate to meet Randi Weingarten, a world-class human being, educator, attorney, and labor leader who went on to become president of the United Federation of Teachers and subsequently the

American Federation of Teachers. Because my appreciation for the work of educators was already in my tackle box, I could speak her language and cultivate the expertise for her membership's investment needs. Plus, in my tackle box was an understanding of the principles of organized labor—thanks to my uncles, who were all proud union members. Having those experiences came in handy for investing the union pensions of millions of educators. My work on behalf of three million members of the National Education Association absolutely elevated Gardner Rich & Company to world-class stature.

Every year, when the NEA held their annual conference, I tried to outdo myself with a show of gratitude. My mother, my number-one teacher, had prioritized all forms of good manners—starting with gratitude. She would remind me that there are three phrases in the English language that take almost no effort to say and that can be more powerful than high-level diplomacy: "Please," "Thank you," and "I'm sorry." World-class manners is no small item to carry around in your tackle box. The way I said "Thank you" to the NEA members was to present awards of money to one or two unsung teachers at their conference each year and to throw big parties for everyone else. The most fun of it for me was selecting the top entertainment from the music world. Well, because of all that time aspiring to be Miles Davis and trying to develop world-class skills at playing jazz, I brought in some of the coolest artists to perform. Those tastes and talents for finding the best entertainment were also in my tackle box.

Then there were the lessons from homelessness and other challenging experiences in my life that definitely had led to the development of world-class skills, talent, and expertise.

Our driver shared the fact that he had been through rough times and wondered if the things he'd learned could be in his tackle box.

"Yes, absolutely," I assured him. "You could be on your way to world-class toughness or resilience or better instincts. Or world-class kindness. Or patience. When you do an inventory of those lessons, you'll be surprised by how much valuable stuff is in there."

The best example I could offer was an opportunity I'd been given not long ago to consult for a major municipal transit system.

Brooke guessed where this was going. "BART?" she blurted out.

"Yes, BART!" I acknowledged. When I went to the meeting, I didn't exactly say that there was a time when I was homeless and used to live on BART with my toddler son. However, when we started talking about every facet of operation of the different lines and the exact amount of time it took to travel from one station to the next, they were floored by my world-class expertise.

A light of understanding came over Brooke's face. "Oh, now I get it when you say skills are transferable. How are dreams transferable?"

"Good question," said our driver.

To answer it, I decided to return to portions of a story aired earlier and to enlist the help of my protégé.

★ ★ ★

It bears repeating that my entire career in the arena of Wall Street was made possible by a poster at the recruiting center in Milwaukee that promised JOIN THE NAVY . . . SEE THE WORLD. Aside from my dream to become world-class at something one day, I could not have been more motivated than by the desire for travel and the need to get as far away as possible from Milwaukee.

Brooke reminded me, "And you had just come from seeing *The Last Detail* with Jack Nicholson and you loved the uniform." She knew the story well.

In my imagination, I dreamt of tossing my seabag over the side of a famous Navy battleship, hopping aboard, and sailing off to distant shores. Instead, I had to go to Navy boot camp first, and then, for my specialization as a medic, I wound up right here in Illinois at the Great Lakes training center—ninety minutes from Milwaukee. What a letdown. But sometimes those letdowns, detours, and disappointments lead you to exactly where you need to be to develop those world-class skills necessary for you to advance to the next place in your journey.

When I reviewed my opportunities in the Navy, the first thing that popped out was becoming a medic. This was my first instance of recognizing that skills could be transferable.

Brooke explained to our driver, "That's because his first real job was as an orderly at Hearthside Nursing Home, and he got some skills there."

Pushing wheelchairs and dealing with bedpans didn't feel like anything that would require talent or expertise, but the real experience I was given was in helping the elderly get fed, bathed, and respected. There was one gentleman, well advanced in his cognitive decline, who barely remembered his own family, but he bonded with me somehow. Whenever I'd come to feed him or change his bedding, he would salute and mumble a greeting. He knew something about my future that even I didn't know. The job taught me patience and focus, and gave me a foundation for understanding medicine. My skills transferred easily toward the medic training I received in the Navy, and I graduated at the top of my class—which entitled me to fill out what was called a "dream sheet."

Brooke hadn't heard this part yet but was eager to know what a dream sheet was.

For the top graduates of the medic training program this happened to be a wish list we filled out with our first, second, and third choices of where we hoped to be stationed. I went for three of the warmest, most tropical getaway locations I could find: Hawaii, the Bahamas, and Japan. Assured of at least one of those spots, I decided to go out with some of the guys to celebrate shortly before receiving my actual assignment. Bad idea. When I got caught sneaking back onto the base after curfew, there went my eligibility to be stationed at one of those dream destinations. Instead, I was shipped off to Camp Lejeune in Jacksonville, North Carolina.

Brooke hadn't heard about this self-sabotage. Her look of disappointment prompted me to say, "It was a good thing. Because even your mistakes and your missteps give you lessons and expertise that are useful later on." Besides, I continued, Camp Lejeune was exactly where I was supposed to be. It was there that I met the world-class heart surgeon who later brought me out to San Francisco. It was there that I learned things and got some experiences that I would have never gotten had I not been at that place at that point in my life.

In learning that skills could be transferable, I had found the key to making them world-class skills. "You transfer them to do something you are even more passionate about."

Our driver glanced over his shoulder. He still had a question:

"What's supposed to happen when you work two jobs, you got no money, no time to go to college to get the skills to transfer?"

I had heard all varieties of that concern everywhere I traveled. This was the classic Catch-22, and I'd thought about alternatives. One young woman who worked her way up at the office of the nurse's union had always dreamt of being an RN but couldn't find the means to get the training. Once she decided to go in search of a solution, she found out the union had a program that would pay for her to go back to school while she was still working.

Then there was a young man I met who was a desk clerk at a hotel, but that wasn't his dream. He confided in me that he had grown up wanting to be a world-famous chef and one day open up his own restaurant. My suggestion to him was to explore the possibility of joining the military.

Brooke instantly asked, "What did he say?"

"That young man looked at me like I had two heads!" But he did stop to listen when I reported that *every* job that exists in the civilian world exists in the military. On an aircraft carrier, say the USS *Abraham Lincoln*, there are four thousand sailors who have to be fed four meals a day. Do the math. As a cook on that ship, you'd be serving sixteen thousand meals a day!

We can take that a step further. Let's say the ship is at sea for six months—180 days, how many meals is that? It's 2,880,000! If this young man went the Navy route, he would not only develop superior cooking skills, he would also have exceptional expertise in time management, asset allocation, and event planning. For someone dreaming of being world-class as a chef and restaurant owner, that path was all upsides.

"Do you see how skills and dreams are equally transferable?"

"Yes!" both Brooke and our driver answered in unison.

"You know where I really developed world-class skills?" I winked at my granddaughter because she knew what was coming.

"You were the . . . um . . . proctology expert."

"Exactly. We don't have to go into details, but let's just say I started at the bottom. Camp Lejeune, in those days, was the largest Marine Corps base in the world! Sixty thousand Marines! That's a lot of bottoms! I got a lot of practice!"

"Poppa!" Brooke groaned. Our driver cracked up.

I was serious. If you want to understand people and how to talk to them and listen to them, proctology is the best way to develop those skills. I became so good at my job that I could drain an abscess and eat lunch at the same time.

Brooke and our driver groaned together this time.

Nothing in the absolute universe of experience could have better prepared me for the demanding range of people I would meet once I got to Wall Street. Nobody could show me anything I had not seen before.

Yep, dealing with stressed-out people is a major transferable skill. One of the most memorable incidents was the time when a super A-type Marine pilot, a full-bird colonel—the kind with all the medals and awards—came in to see me on a Friday with a major problem. Before I could even do a procedure, I said, "We're going to have to get the swelling down. I'll get you some suppositories to take, and you can have a sitz bath. That should relieve the swelling and help you get comfortable enough to have a bowel movement. Come back and see me on Monday."

When he left, he seemed to have relaxed somewhat so I was

surprised on Monday when he came storming in, along with his wife, yelling about seeing my commanding officer. Both of them were looking at me like *You're not a real doctor! You're Black too!* This colonel was so irate he was going to have me written up and replaced. My commanding officer happened to be busy at the moment, so the colonel and his wife had to sit there and steam in the waiting room. Finally he lost it, jumped up, and confronted me, saying, "You don't know what the hell you're doing. You shouldn't be here! For all the good those pills did me I may as well have been sticking them up my ass!"

The self-control required for me to not laugh out loud was intense. He had taken rectal suppositories by mouth. No wonder his ass was still hurting. Politely and calmly I showed him the directions on the suppository package, explaining, "Sir, those pills you took? You *are* supposed to stick them up your ass to relieve the pain and swelling." His wife at that point appeared to want to say *I told you so* but refrained.

He retracted his plan to have me written up, and I lived to tell the tale. That lesson I learned in not overreacting went into my tackle box to be used countless times in my dealings at every level of my Wall Street career. I dealt with a client on the phone for years, a Texas oilman who had no idea that I was African American and who managed to tell me the most racist, offensive jokes you can even imagine. Whenever I've talked about that client in recent years, I've been criticized for not reporting him or at least refusing to be subjected to a hostile work environment.

While I get it and am supportive of anyone who speaks out against overt or covert racist rhetoric—whether purposely threatening, accidental, or even the kind expressed through unconscious micro-aggressions—I didn't have the luxury to lose the business. As I explained to our cabdriver and my granddaughter, "It was not my time for me to sing 'We shall overcome.' I had just finished clawing and scratching my way out of the gutter, with a baby tied on my back. It was time to get paid . . ."

Many times I wanted nothing more than to hang up, but I had something else to prove. If I was going to be world-class at making money for clients, I challenged myself to one day reveal the truth to this oilman and then find out what mattered to him. Would he choose to hold on to his racist ignorance or change his bias thanks to the most impressive return on the dollar I was getting him?

To say that this Texas oilman was shocked when we met for the first time would be an understatement. Believe it or not, as he stood and gawked at me, trying to gather his words, he had an old-fashioned smackdown delivered by the hand of God. He seemed to like me *more*. No, he was not cured of his racist ways completely, but I think he changed somewhat. In fact, he probably thought twice about deriving pleasure from telling jokes based on racial stereotypes. With me, from then on, he switched it up and starting telling—wait for it—knock-knock jokes!

The moral of the story is that this wasn't a matter of black or white. It was a matter of green.

"Yeah," our driver said. "It's all about the Benjamins."

"Oh, *that* green," Brooke chimed in.

Green is powerful. I was making money for that man, changing some of his bigotry, and boosting my skills and income by handling his account. From time immemorial, different groups of people with biases and prejudices have come together for mutual betterment—as trading partners, as cohabitants of neighborhoods and of the shrinking ground of Planet Earth.

That lesson about the power of green was yet another reason why I came to believe that we needed to be teaching financial literacy at an earlier age to encourage more young people of color to pursue careers in the business world. Again, all the experiences stored in my tackle box helped me develop the expertise that helped me realize the dream of opening up my own firm and of becoming a world-class entrepreneur. Those skills were mostly thanks to the Navy and, indirectly, proctology.

There was one other important transferrable skill and dream that I took with me from the Navy to my surgical and research training at the Veterans Administration, and then transferred it to my own Wall Street business and beyond. It was a belief in the value of public service. As the years have gone by, I've become increasingly grateful for having been given the chance to serve my country in uniform. Not everyone is cut out for military service, but I have long felt that every citizen should spend a couple of years serving in a capacity that makes a difference to others—whether in the armed forces or with the Peace Corps, Teach For America, Habitat for Humanity, or any one of the many organizations grappling with the effects of climate change or helping rebuild communities after environmental disasters. Even in our most difficult economic periods, I believe our country's greatest national resources are our *human* resources: our diverse, multi-cultural, multi-ethnic, multi-geographical workforce. The skills, talent, and expertise we have in our collective tackle box are all transferrable too.

I wrapped up my explanation by saying, "That's the beautiful thing about the transference of dreams that start out small, even insignificant. You can forget about them and then wake up one day and they've transformed into something else much bigger."

My phone, which our driver had been kind enough to re-charge, had somehow turned itself on and began to chirp madly, a telltale sign that I had voice and text messages piling up. He handed the phone back to me and I promptly turned it off. There was more to say about world-class skills.

* * *

As we closed in on our destination, our driver commented that he thought more people should take the time to really look at their tackle box, to see what was going on in there. He made me think of something else—that it's also important to keep your skills and talents up to date. Clearly technology had been kicking my butt all day. We had almost gotten stranded Beyond the Wall with a dead phone. Most cabdrivers in Chicago like ours keep their regular taxi businesses and drive for the vehicle-hire apps too. Everybody is grinding. Everybody has to stay relevant.

As a matter of fact, for all of us who didn't spend our forma-tive years with screens in our hands and in front of us, but who are now forced to reinvent ourselves, permission to dream may require brush-up courses and treks back to school. If I had learned anything about staying young and current, about keeping up to date with technology and culture, I had to credit the person who inspired that awareness in me the most: none other than the late Dr. Maya Angelou. She could quote Aristotle and Jay Z in the same breath. She could dance the foxtrot and teach you how to Dougie.

Dr. Angelou was the one who convinced me that at every age we're always refining, transposing, and reinventing our dreams. For example, when I told her about my wanting to be Miles Davis and how intensely I'd wanted to become world-class at the trumpet, Dr. Angelou told me, "You *are* Miles Davis. You just are playing a different instrument."

During the first year after Holly's death, I visited Maya Angelou frequently at her home in North Carolina. She too knew that her days were numbered. Yet she laughed her rich, melodious laugh when I told her about Atomic Time and how Holly had mistaken the word "automatic" for "atomic." She agreed with Holly's assertion that I needed to decide what I wanted to do with my most precious resource of time. Maya worried about the pace of my speaking schedule and that I had not allowed myself to fully grieve.

Brooke had heard about my final visits with Dr. Angelou, but I realized that she might not have ever heard the story of how, as a little girl, Maya had stopped talking for five years of her life. Carefully I recounted the broad strokes of the trauma Maya suffered at the age of eight—of being raped by her mother's boyfriend and, after reporting what had happened, coming to the false conclusion that her voice of truth was to blame for the man being beaten to death.

For those five years she stayed almost completely silent, except for a few words spoken to her brother. In that time, she was fortunate to have had a teacher who encouraged her to go to the library and read history and literature written by the world-class masters of every genre. "Just imagine how studying the world-class skills of novelists, playwrights, historians, philosophers, political writers, and poets helped her develop her own skills and talents. You can only imagine how her dreams of being able to do what they did must have carried her through." When she finally spoke again, her teacher encouraged her to read her poetry aloud because that was the only way to hear her own music. From then on, Maya always had something to say.

Talk about transferable skills, talent, and expertise. Talk about transferable dreams.

Any attempt to narrow the realizations of Dr. Angelou's dreams to one arena would be impossible. She wrote thirty-six books, thirty of which were bestsellers. An award-winning poet, memoirist, and journalist, she also wrote essays, plays, and movie and television scripts. Plus, she was a spectacular actress, director, producer, dancer, and singer (in the 1950's she had a small role in the opera *Porgy and Bess* that toured the world). She was a prominent civil rights activist who worked alongside Dr. King and the SCLC as well as with Malcolm X. And she was a college professor who received more than seventy-three honorary degrees.

In all that time she spent at the library, dreaming and traveling in her mind, Dr. Maya Angelou taught herself to believe in removing all limitations as to what was possible. In her late teens, when her mother relocated the family to San Francisco, Maya set her sights on becoming the first Black streetcar conductor. Why? What possessed her to be world-class at driving a streetcar? Apparently it was the uniform! And she did it. Hey, I could relate. Dreams have to start somewhere.

Brooke sat up in her seat, astounded. "You never told me she did all that. And it all began by going to the library?"

Without answering her, I had a flash of a memory and also sat up in my seat. "You know what your great-grandmother used to tell me about the public library? She said it was the most dangerous place possible because you could go in there and learn how to do anything. You want to be world-class, go to the library. Everything you learn will accumulate in your tackle box."

For a moment or two I had to take a break and close my eyes, inhale a deep breath, and fill up with memories of three of my most important life influences, all no longer with us: Uncle Henry; my mother, Bettye Jean Gardner Triplett; and Dr. Maya Angelou.

When I opened my eyes again, those memories floated away and I heard Holly's voice, reminding me that time was a-wasting. What was I going to do with the Atomic Time that was left to me?

For someone who'd been gone almost five years, she sounded as present as ever, saying as clear as day, *Tell me.*

EIGHT

THE REP,
THE RAP,
AND
THE ROLODEX

Just to prove how transformed I really was, I decided to have our driver take us back to the music store. We were going Beyond the Wall *again*. Outside it looked like Siberia still, but all precipitation had ceased. At two p.m. on a weekday, the frozen barren streets looked ready for two Abominable Snowmen to show up and have a showdown.

This last detour was a suggestion from my granddaughter. She explained that her hunger had subsided for the time being and she wanted to make sure we could retrace our steps—in case we ever needed to come back again. At first I resisted but then went for it. Why not? This way I'd have one more opportunity to face down something I had allowed myself to fear unnecessarily for so long. The unknown was now slightly more known.

Our return to the North would also give us an extra fifteen minutes, during which I could explain another useful technique for communicating, selling, and/or advancing your dream. It's a tool, I announced, made possible by brushing up on the 3R's.

"Brush up on them?" Brooke asked. "Well, what are they?"

"You don't know? They didn't teach you that song?"

Our driver wasn't sure either. But then he remembered his grandparents asking about his schoolwork and something about the 3R's.

Now they were making me feel ancient. Let's just say folks my age and older recall the original 3R's—Reading, wRiting, and aRithmetic. The phrase may have come to us from a toast given at a dinner by Sir William Curtis in 1795, and then a song mentioning them came along about one hundred years later that we all had to sing.

"So," I announced, "there's a new 3R's that was composed by yours truly and I'm referring to the Rep, the Rap, and the Rolodex."

Having captured their attention, I gave them the breakdown. In order.

If you want to present your dream, your plan, your need for investment or support, or share your vision to gain guidance, supporters, followers, and fans, the 3R's are indispensable. Simply stated, the questions this new set of R's covers are: *who* is the dreamer, *what* best communicates the dream, and *how* does the dream connect to others?

THE REP

It's important to have a reputation for excellence in both your business and your personal relationships. What do people say about you when you're not in the room? Never compromise your reputation. Once it's compromised, it's hard to restore. You can come in tainted, or you can come in shining like a ROCK STAR! It's never too early to begin creating, living, or brandishing a stellar reputation.

THE RAP

You've got to be able to communicate in whatever and all mediums. You can have the best goods, services, or products in the world, but if you can't communicate your idea, you'll never sell it!

THE ROLODEX

As I had to explain to Brooke and our driver, the Rolodex—aka a rolling index file—is what we all used to have in our offices before smart phones. It's your contact list, and what I'm really talking about here are relationships, which can be more important than money, on a number of levels. My dreams have been turned real, totally, because of my relationships.

Some dreams don't have to be shared, sold, or communicated, it's true; however, when it comes to creating the reality of dreams that involve competition with others, they do. Yet I assured Brooke and our driver that competition can be your friend.

Brooke puzzled over that for a moment and then agreed. "You could be right. You know in a championship, only one person can be the MVP."

"Correct." I then told them that in a competitive arena where everyone is basically good, there is only so much space separating you from your biggest competitor. In that context, your Rolodex—your relationships—is your most valuable asset of the 3R's. I offered some examples.

Relationships took Gardner Rich & Company to the Big Leagues. We came from nowhere but were allowed to participate in billions of dollars in securities transactions because I'd created relationships all along. They are what allowed me knowledge of and access to the capital and balance sheets of some of the largest investment banks on Wall Street.

Relationships, no matter what your field or focus, can help you gain traction and momentum. It's relationships that, with a phone call, can ease or force doors open that others may choose to close.

Relationships give you the inside track too. Information can be the coin of the realm in certain industries. Knowing who's who can give you an edge. Then you'll know who can jerk whose chain if needed.

Again, in a world of global competition, where everyone on the playing field is good and where opportunities may be scarce, the person who will achieve his or her dream is the one who has created, nurtured, invested in, treasured, and protected the best relationships.

I was so excited to share the 3R's it hadn't even occurred to me to worry about us being back up in uncharted territory in this part of town.

Brooke turned her head to look at me half amused, half surprised. "Really, Poppa Bear?" she challenged. "The Rep, the Rap, and the Rolodex mean that much?"

Without hesitating, I replied, "Take me right now. Take all of the assets away. Just give me the new 3R's. I'd be like Bruno Mars. 'Don't Believe Me Just Watch!'"

Our driver had that song on his playlist and fired it up. We broke out on the chorus, all of us singing.

Outside the window of the cab, nothing looked familiar. Were we getting lost again?

Brooke protectively steered my attention back to the 3R's, asking where they had come from.

Some years ago, I answered her, an opportunity had arisen to meet with a group of veterans of different ages. Most had experienced homelessness and joblessness but were getting their lives back on track, starting with the permission to dream. Some were entering the civilian workforce for the first time; others were focused on developing underused skills they'd overlooked in their tackle box; still others hoped to launch businesses of their own or retrain for entirely new careers. Many of them really wanted to know from me how to put themselves out there in front of others—for job interviews or when meeting prospective investors. All of them wanted to know how to open the right doors, say the right things, and connect to the right people.

The Rep, the Rap, and the Rolodex was something I had been applying all along, but I'd never had to break it down before I met this group of vets and we'd had our meeting. They also helped me see something that I'd missed. Your Rolodex of relationships should not only contain connections to the right people who can help you. It should also contain connections to the right people you can help.

Our driver spontaneously said, "That right there is powerful." He asked if I wouldn't mind reviewing the Rep and the Rap.

Brooke egged me on too.

Your Rep was something, I insisted, that not enough young people really understood. In many businesses, for example, a book gets compiled about you. In politics or government jobs, in the age of the internet, these books get assembled fast. Even before Google or other search engines, on Wall Street and in various corporate settings this book, containing records of your past performance, could be checked.

"Take sports," I continued. "When the pitcher steps up to the mound to face a batter, there's a whole book on the hitting rep of that player that the pitcher has already studied. A world-class pitcher would know from the book that this guy will chase a ball on the outside or that he won't swing at anything in one sliver of the strike zone or he's susceptible to a fastball."

It used to be that many job recruiters would put together data to create books on applicants. That's changed with the advent of social media. If you're a young dreamer who aspires to be world-class in a professional context, you might forget that there is now a book on you compiled from all of your social media activity. You might have the best résumé and a stellar academic record that shows you graduated at the top of your class. You might've worked at the top of your game for years in a few industries. Maybe you have impeccable letters from your professors and employers and coworkers. You can be a rock star in an interview, but the minute you walk out of that room, the first place human resources or other decision makers go is straight to your social media profiles. You might have thought that witty comment you made on Twitter was harmless, but it's not if you're going to work for that company. Maybe there's a selfie of you chugging a drink at that frat party or a video of you shaking your behind in a club. None of these things are terrible marks of low character, but if you want others to be part of your journey toward advancing your dream, it's best to make sure your Rep is ready for primetime.

It's harsh but necessary to say this to young people—as well as to older folks—but you almost want to Mirandize yourself before you go anywhere. Remember that what you say and do can and will be used against you. We should all have a time in our lives when we act foolish and say or do things we later wish we hadn't. However, in a time when there are eyes in the skies on us 24/7, with everyone filming everything, those foolish days will cause problems. Your reputation can be easily harmed and hard to repair. Just an accusation or rumor can have a shelf life like nuclear waste, and you will glow in the dark for a very long time.

When prospective employers or investors are wowed by your world-class skills or your promise of developing them and you are welcomed aboard their company, remind yourself every day to act in a way that would make the person you admire most feel proud of you.

"Well, in that case, I know who the person I'll think about is . . ." Brooke began.

"Who, me?" I said, joking a little but not entirely.

"No, Poppa, you're number two. I have to go with President Obama."

Priceless. I was number two after President Obama, who had been out of office for almost two years at that point and was desperately missed by us. My question to Brooke was if she remembered what the president had said to her when we went to the Oval Office and she sat at the Big Desk.

"I do. He said, 'If you do real good in school and you do everything your grandpoppa says, in thirty years maybe this office could be yours.'" I was about to remind Brooke of her response when she continued, "And I told him that it was going to be twenty-seven and a half years because I was already seven and a half."

I had never forgotten the look I received from Barack Obama. He was impressed. She was serious.

"Good, so as you dream every day about becoming president of the United States, you'll start to carry yourself with that stature and not want to do something or say something or post something that might come back to haunt you."

Brooke solemnly nodded. If there ever was a preferred time to talk to someone about taking care of their Rep, I say the younger the better. She definitely took my words to heart.

Once you know the skills, talent, and expertise you have in your tackle box, and once you have done your best to protect your reputation, the second R is the Rap—or how you communicate who you are and the substance of your dreams, ideas, plans, and goals to the marketplace. In the olden days, you had a résumé, and if you were pitching a company or a business investment, you had marketing materials and a well-conceived business plan. Creative, innovative, and entrepreneurial dreamers these days have websites, social media presences, streaming interviews, their own YouTube channels—you name it.

These tools are really double-edged swords. On the one hand, there are opportunities to gain large followings through social media and even to monetize your content online. Entertainers who can make funny videos or have real world-class talent as musicians or singers or self-help motivational gurus can all use a Rap to define themselves and draw traffic. Content creators of every background compete wildly to become influencers, and some do. Many social entrepreneurs and political activists have powerful messaging that sometimes cuts through the relentless flow of information bombarding us at every turn, trying to drag us into one more click. Using your Rap online to build a business or a following is a little like being a billboard for advertisers. As long as you're clear about what you're selling, it's an opportunity to explore.

On the other hand, your ability to communicate your dream to others will almost always have the most impact if you can look into someone's eyes or stand in front of them and be able to move them emotionally. You may think that a Rap is a monologue, but in my experience it's meant to be an exchange. You have to be able to read a person's reactions to make sure you're connecting to them.

Everyone used to talk about honing their "elevator pitch," which they should still talk about. The ability to say everything you would like to say in a forty-five-minute presentation but squeezed into three minutes is like bottled lightning. You grab a person's attention, tell them what you have that is of interest to them, give them the "high concept" of your pitch (one or two lines that distill it to its most provocative elements), and hand them your card. Some of my biggest breaks happened in literal elevator pitches.

If you have more than three minutes, use the extra time to talk a little about your Rep—not just your accomplishments but also your values, your passions, and your larger dreams, which might include others. I like to think of your Rep as your past, your Rap as your present, including your biggest dream, and your Rolodex as your past, present, and future combined. Transforming your dream into a reality is not something that takes place in a vacuum. You'll need others to sign on in one form or another—yet again why the Rolodex matters so much.

Our driver had now gotten lost. He apologized profusely, thinking that maybe he had not been paying close enough attention. We tried all the same technology tricks we had used earlier in the day, but somehow we couldn't find the same music store.

Later on, I'd go looking for the store again—in my own car—and not be able to find it either. I couldn't remember the name or the address. Almost as if it had all been a dream. But Brooke had her harmonica and remembered most of the same details. The other name that evaded my memory was that of our driver. I'm sure at some point he had told me, but it had vanished from my brain like the name of the musical instrument store.

By the way, I am a world-class name rememberer. Through-out the years I have developed true tricks of the trade for never forgetting a name. President Bill Clinton was world-class at re-membering names—he could meet you in a receiving line in 1992 and spot you again at a conference on globalization ten years later, say your name, and pick up on the same conversa-tion you'd had a decade before. For anyone hoping to build a meaningful Rolodex, remembering names is a talent that makes people feel good.

Something about that trip Beyond the Wall must have put me in an altered state. Not just the names of the store and our driver were lost in my memory vault. Whenever I thought back to the events of the day, they formed a dreamy, wintery blur. Everything seemed to have been mysteriously orchestrated for me and Brooke to have this long and comprehensive conversation.

After finally conceding that we had failed in our search for the elusive world-class musical instrument shop, I decided we needed to get back to the restaurant before it closed. As we made our way there, Brooke wanted to make sure I didn't lose my train of thought on the 3R's.

I was just getting to the most important part about the Rolo-dex, I promised. The number-one best piece of advice I would give anyone who wants to create a circle of influence, a network, or a following is that the best time to make friends is before you need friends. Likewise the best time to make connections is before you need connections. And finding opportunities and making con-nections does not happen on a website or with an app. "Also, don't forget that friends and connections are not just folks you think can help you but maybe folks you can help."

Bottom line: relationships are to be treasured, protected, and a part of your dreams.

Brooke couldn't hold back from asking if I had just one story about putting the 3R's to use for making my dreams real. Boy, did I ever.

* * *

I set the scene: "There I was, still in New York but thinking about trying to start a business and looking for ideas. The big question in my mind was *How do I get in front of some people?* My Rep was solid from my San Francisco and New York track records, and I was working on some strong talking points for my rap."

"But no Rolodex?" Brooke asked, surprised.

"I was working on it, but these were early days." So I got on my rotary-dial phone and began calling a list of CEOs from every industry and then started to pay attention to a list of the largest Black-owned businesses in the country. On that list was the nation's number-one, largest and oldest Black-owned life insurance institution: North Carolina Mutual Life Insurance in lovely downtown Durham, North Carolina. My phone call went through, and I had a conversation with the chief investment officer. The plan was to make a connection and continue talking about investment opportunities over time. Although I called back a few more times, I could never get him on the phone again—for whatever reason.

In the meantime, I had been making call after call to other names on the list, not giving up, making some connections, but nothing had yielded much promise. Out of frustration, one afternoon I called North Carolina Mutual Life Insurance back and decided to ask for the office of the chairman of the board,

W. J. Kennedy III. Not surprisingly, I didn't get through to him, but I did leave a message. Surprisingly, he called back—and got straight down to business, wanting to know the nature of my phone call to him.

Well, what I said was "I called your chief investment officer last month with a recommendation. He did not take my recommendation. However, had he taken it, I would be writing you a check right now for two hundred fifty thousand dollars."

Mr. Kennedy paused. Then he said, "Son, you need to come down here and see me."

Needless to say, I was on the next thing smokin' down to North Carolina.

W. J. Kennedy III was the grandson of the founder of the company and a very high profile member of his community in Durham, North Carolina—which at one point in time had been designated as the Black Wall Street. This was old wealth for the lineages of several African American firms that were over a hundred years old.

W. J. Kennedy III was world-class in every way and one of the most remarkably intelligent people I'd ever met. He had not one but two MBAs—one from Wharton and the other from NYU. He had served in the US Army and sat on the board of directors of Fortune 500 companies such as Quaker Oats, Mobile Corporation, and Pfizer, to name a few.

I admitted to being in awe of Mr. Kennedy's larger-than-life presence that first time we met. A giant of a man who stood about six foot six and was at least three hundred pounds, he shook my hand and I felt as if I were shaking hands with a bear. We hit it off from the word go. We sat down and talked about his life, his work, my interests, my life, and my dreams to one day have a firm of my own. Sometimes all the Rap you need is just being your authentic self without trying to sell anything. Mr. Kennedy not only became an account, he soon also became a mentor. Our relationship strengthened even more when I left Bear Stearns for Chicago, and during my lean days, he wrote me a check for ten thousand dollars. No strings, no questions asked. When I needed some doors opened at places like Pfizer, Quaker Oats, and Mobile, he was happy to help. More important to my cause, though, was his uncanny guidance for over twenty years.

My first presentation to the powers-that-be at Quaker Oats convinced me W. J. Kennedy was a Jedi. The energy was testy. Clearly they had only taken the meeting because Kennedy had asked on my behalf. Usually in those situations you go in, it's pro forma, everyone's chitchatty, and nobody can wait to tear out of there. Nobody bothered even chatting this time. My Rep and my Rap were of no help. After getting an initial feel for their needs, I had to really PUSH for the subsequent meeting, but nobody was committing. Mr. Kennedy, again, made a call, set up the meeting for me, but this time he gave me a specific question to ask about their numbers, and the moment I did, all of a sudden *everything* shifted. The power and the energy in the room started to flow. The executives in the meeting were masters of the universe and they did not expect me to ask something that only a psychic genius could know. They were awestruck.

Naturally Mr. Kennedy didn't tell me the answer. He just said to ask the question. No problem. The power shifted, and I now was talking to these movers and shakers as a peer.

"Whoa," our driver had to say. "I get it."

Brooke added, "I gotta get to work on my 3R's, Poppa."

One of the lessons I most hoped she would remember from this day was from this last story: that nothing really comes to those who are afraid to ask. What begins with a dream—whether the dream is for yourself or for someone you love, for your community, for your country, or for your world—has to be spoken into existence. If you're dreaming of pancakes and bacon, by all means, put out the word. If you're dreaming of meaningful relationships, both personal and professional, put out the word.

When you're willing to ask the universe or whoever your higher power is, you may not always get what you want, but as the Rolling Stones told us, you'll get what you need.

NINE

THIS HAS BEEN DONE BEFORE

Before we left the cab for good, Brooke asked, what was the hardest thing about turning dreams into reality. She made her question sound like I might have a fast and easy answer.

"That's a great, great question," I began. "Because it reveals the reason that people get stuck or lost or whatever it is that happens to prevent them from continuing to give themselves permission to dream." I went on to say that what they forget is that we all have a treasure map, so to speak, that we've inherited. It shows us how others have dealt with similar difficulties and managed to achieve the impossible against all odds.

"You don't mean a real treasure map, right?" Brooke felt free to ask the obvious, just in case. "Does everybody inherit it?"

"Yes, everyone has a treasure map inside. It's the knowledge that everything we dream has been turned into reality before. Everything that seems impossible to overcome or to achieve has been done before."

This treasure map, I explained, could be found in our collective human DNA—something I call spiritual genetics—and it gives us our moral compass, our confidence, and our courage. The beautiful thing is that unlike our physical genetics, which we inherit without choice, we get to choose whose spiritual genetics we want. Instead of the spiritual genetics of my father and the cycle of men who abandon their children, I embraced the spiritual genetics of my mother and of others who inspire me and with whom I do not share a single drop of blood.

The mood in the car changed, kind of the way a trumpet solo by Miles Davis can make you feel that your atomic structure was being changed.

Our driver asked whether that would mean, since he was adopted, he shared the spiritual genetics of his adoptive parents. And both Brooke and I nodded our heads at once.

"We're all family here. The inheritance that we choose to embrace can come from those who've lived and died, and who we never met, and who aren't blood relatives to us." That is our treasure map.

Something else about spiritual genetics is that familiar feeling you have when you meet someone for the first time but it feels like you've known that person forever. Like déjà vu, or as I translated for Brooke, "Already seen." It's because you're a match in your spiritual genetics—you're old-soul relatives.

This seemed like as good a time as any to tell Brooke a story about how I first got to know her favorite role model, Barack Obama. At the time, Barack was a state senator getting ready to run for the US Senate. My business was well established, and for the first time I had been talking publicly about my past and about overcoming homelessness—which was leading to opportunities I had never imagined. Folks were talking about book and film deals. Offers of public-speaking engagements had begun to come in.

"It turned out that Barack Obama, elected to the US Senate in 2004, and I worked out at the same gym with the same phenomenal trainer, Cornell McClellan." That's how we became friends. At the gym, we'd work out, talk briefly here and there, but something about him made him seem like family. Both of us had been raised in single-mother households—although in much different circumstances. Our paths had taken us in different directions, but as he later said to me, one thing we definitely had in common was "Nobody saw us coming."

One day at the gym we stopped our workouts to talk, and that's when Senator Obama mentioned that the rumblings were true and he was going to run for president. "Cool," I said. "I'm going into the movie business."

"Cool," said the future 44th president of the United States of America.

Cornell wasted no time. He walked over to us and stood, arms akimbo, and said in his most commanding voice, "Ain't nobody going anywhere till you finish your workout."

The future President Obama and I did not question Cornell. We went back to our workouts and then had to hurry off to the demands of turning our dreams into reality. His involved overcoming extraordinary, impossible odds, but he never forgot that he was walking in the footsteps of others who had come before him. They might not have been the first African American to be elected president of the United States of America, but he knew that feats as improbable as his had been done before.

Brooke proudly proclaimed about that story, "You both had the audacity!"

She was right. And President Obama also had the audacity to take Cornell to Washington, DC, with him, and I sorely missed his world-class training expertise. But Brooke was right: it takes audacity to dream. In good times, it takes audacity to dream, without a doubt. Oh, but when things are crazy, unprecedented, and uncertain, as they were going to become—on steroids—within a few years, it takes something more: the treasure map, the spiritual inheritance of those who have faced darkness and chosen to become the light.

In those times, we step up or we fall. There is a pronounced memory I have of talking to Dr. Angelou at one point about fears, challenges, and pain. This was just the beginning of me asking myself some big questions, not just about my future or my family's future but about the future of our country. My horizons were changing, and I wanted to know what my role could be in helping to create, facilitate, and lead an unfolding journey of a collective dream.

It was right then, as we sat and talked, that Dr. Angelou said to me, "We must all remember that we have the people for this mountain."

A weight lifted from me after hearing that one statement.

She went further. "We should all be mindful of the fact that there were those who came before us, who came up a steeper side of this mountain with little or no opportunity, but they kept going forward, upward, and onward! *And still I rise!*"

The power of telling yourself, "This has been done before," can ease more burdens than I am able to count—whether you are dealing with a personal or a global struggle.

"This has been done before" is what you tell yourself when adverse circumstances collide with your dreams and cause you to fear you'll never crawl your way out of that place. "This has been done before" is what spurs on movements of people dreaming of freedom and equality.

Dr. Angelou's message was a call to action. In a time when so many worry that the next generations will be among the first not to do better than their parents, when a lot of people question whether we will ever attain the American Dream, she recognized that a hard pivot was in order. She was goading me, reminding me that our spiritual genetics, our internal treasure maps, could guide us toward reinvention and toward reclaiming dreams that had ostensibly become out of reach.

The hardest part of turning dreams into reality, I answered Brooke, is forgetting that someone came before you to make the realization of your dreams possible.

In our collective human history, we have always had people for our toughest and most treacherous mountains.

With a wink at Brooke, I asked our driver if he minded my asking him a question.

"Me?"

I was curious, I said, what he considered to be the greatest export in the history of the United States.

Brooke saw where this was going. She played along. "Manufacturing?" she asked.

"No!"

"Technology?" our driver asked.

"No!"

"Hamburgers?" our driver tried.

"Naw."

Brooke was happy to state the answer that she knew well: "The greatest export in the history of the United States is the American Dream, the belief that you can do or be anything you determine for yourself."

I echoed her. "That *is* the greatest export in the history of the United States."

Our driver glanced back at me and then at Brooke and he just smiled.

In that moment I came out of retirement. True, I had been working but not with heart. From then on, I decided, whenever anyone asked me what kind of new business I was in, I was going to say that I was in the import-export business.

* * *

Our driver tried to refuse my money. He said he had already been paid many times over. He was going home with riches he never knew existed before—his tackle box, a new command of the 3R's, and a treasure map to his inheritance. And, of course, permission to dream.

Naturally, I wouldn't hear of it. Before Brooke and I jumped back out into the cold, I asked for a favor.

"Anything!"

I asked him to find a Beatles song for me on his phone and to put it on his speaker. The song was "All You Need Is Love," written by John Lennon and Paul McCartney. We listened to it twice. The second time, Brooke got out her harmonica and added her own flavor to the musical track. She sounded like a pro! The lyrics were lines you could live by:

There's nothing you can do that can't be done
Nothing you can sing that can't be sung . . .

We sang it all through again after that, each of us letting loose on the part that went, "It's easy . . . !" Because sometimes it really can just be easy—if you dream that it can be so.

Famished by now, as soon as we said our last thank-yous to our driver and disembarked the taxi, Brooke and I decided to have a late lunch at the Four Seasons after all. We had a lot to celebrate. We started to walk in, still humming the tune to the Beatles song. Just before we entered the lobby, we turned back at the same time to wave goodbye to our driver and friend.

POOF! He had vanished into the billowing mist of the darkening afternoon.

Brooke and I looked at each other, mystified. Maybe something had happened to us when we went Beyond the Wall. Maybe the whole day had been a winter mirage or a Chicago North Side hallucination.

Maybe we had changed into wildlings and didn't even know it.

"Well?" Brooke asked me as soon as we were settled at a table and the waiter had taken our order.

To the best of my knowledge, I had not once told her about Holly's question, which had been plaguing me for nearly five years. All day, as far as I could remember, I had not said anything to indicate that, in fact, I finally had my answer.

Yes, you guessed it, I had given myself permission to dream, and I could see its blueprint and a plan and a brand-new chapter that lay ahead of me in this new import-export business, all of it starting the very next day.

Brooke knew. She didn't need me to give her the details. But she knew. All she said was "Just remember, Poppa: one hand, one foot."

If you, like me during that period leading up to that day, ever feel like it's a cruel, cold, hard world out there, it's time to get over it. Time's a-wastin', and this has been done before.

If you gave up or became stuck or don't know how to find your way through the mist to your dream, get out there, Beyond the Wall, past your fears, and begin with the smallest of passing dreams.

You got this. One hand, one foot.

TEN

A MASTERPIECE LIFE

After that day with Brooke, I decided it was time for me—at almost the legal age of retirement—to go back to high school. The next day, I was putting to use all my tools—especially the Rep, the Rap, and the Rolodex—to create a world-class lecture tour that I now call B2HS. My life had transformed in two days.

My wildest dream with B2HS was to visit one hundred high schools and then expand to the rest of the world. We are part of the global family, after all.

The evolution of this dream actually began several years earlier, during a visit to Milwaukee. For some reason I had decided to stop by Lee Elementary School, my old grade school. One of my first memories hit me: the day in 1963 when President John F. Kennedy was assassinated. The wailing on the streets of Milwaukee, at least where I lived, went on for days. Adults some of us had never seen cry were out on the street bent over sobbing. It's true, sometimes through the lens of history, the leaders we most admired happen to have been flawed, and President Kennedy was not an exception. Still, for many of his stances, JFK was a hero. And this was the president who had famously said, "Ask not what your country can do for you but what you can do for your country."

JFK's message stayed with me so strongly throughout my youth. Even as an adult I had often thought, *There's something more I can do. One day.*

Standing in front of Lee Elementary in Milwaukee, so many of those details of childhood remained crisp in my recollections. As the students poured in and out of the school, suddenly an Oprah connection came to mind. As in Winfrey. We have a few things in common, besides having built businesses, brands, and fortunes in Chicago. Oprah Winfrey and I are the same age, the same zodiac sign, and, yes, went to the same elementary school. Reflecting on that, I wondered, *How do we know that the next Chris Gardner, or more importantly the next Oprah Winfrey, is not coming or going through the doors of any public school in the country right now?*

In hindsight I realize the truth is, *they are*! The job I had decided to undertake was to convince them that *they can*! And that's why I took on my newest position and the last job I will ever have. I am now officially the CEO of Happyness, and I love my job!

The more I think about what defines happyness, the more I see it as the joy that comes from knowing you have chosen to be the artist and architect of your own masterpiece life. Being in the business of empowering others to create their own masterpieces is humbling and more rewarding than I ever imagined possible.

You're probably wondering where I got the skills, talent, and expertise to empower younger audiences. Actually, for years I've been a part of different programs aimed at educating inner-city youth in Chicago on such issues as financial literacy. One of them that I helped develop in the '90s, the Summer Finance Academy, became highly popular. During the school year, hearing about me, a teacher I knew asked if I would come to her high school and speak. Now, most people who've known me for the past fifteen years assume that I was born with a silver mic in my hand. Wrong. My public-speaking platform only kicked off in 2006 or so, and this was ten years earlier. Let me tell you, the toughest and most brutal audiences are high school teenagers. They make the audiences up at the Apollo in Harlem look tame by comparison.

Nonetheless, I said yes to the teacher, and when I arrived, already intimidated and nervous, I was informed that my slot was going to be following none other than the late great comedian Bernie Mac. Sweating bullets, I watched him as he blew the roof off the place and had those kids hanging on his every word.

There he was, in the hippest, coolest, boldest, baddest suit made with some kind of shiny purple, yellow, and red fabric, and I was in my conservative business suit. At about that moment I knew I could never be as funny or as flashy as Bernie Mac. All I could do was find that spark of magic that let me be me, and hopefully offer something tangible that could make a difference in their lives.

The good news is that I got out of there alive. The students were, in fact, very receptive, and even though I was no Bernie

Mac, I found out that my comedic timing wasn't terrible. When I told them a little about my story, the parts that seemed to resonate the most were of my own high school days. The important lesson from that experience was that speaking to students was empowering to me. Later, Dr. Angelou gave me the simplest secret to standing up and talking in front of every possible kind of audience. She said, "People might not remember your exact words, but they'll remember how you made them feel."

Nothing could be more evident of her insight than when talking to young people, something I started to do on a fairly regular basis after that first public speaking baptism by fire. Those skills turned out to be transferable. Once I became an author, speaking engagement opportunities skyrocketed. And never stopped.

The moral of that story is there are some dreams you don't have to chase down but will come and find you. Let me encourage you to be receptive to opportunities that may not appear as such in the beginning. When the universe taps you on the shoulder and says there is something you can do for others, guess what—that might by your dream calling you. I tell you this as a reminder to give yourself daily doses of permission to accept the good that is coming to you. I tell you this as a reminder that no matter how young or old you happen to be, you are a child of the universe, loved and meant to be here, a person of worth and substance in this life.

The other moral of the story is how ironic it was that when I decided to go back to high school, I was going back to my roots— the very place where I'd gotten my start as a speaker. From the minute I picked up the phone the day after Brooke and I went out to get her harmonica, everyone I called in my Rolodex wanted to be a part of B2HS—AKA Back 2 High School. That day I booked four schools and a handful of sponsors. Before long, my initial goal of visiting one hundred schools had stretched further.

By the end of the second day, of course, I knew the name of the speech I would be giving on this first of many tours: *Permission to Dream.*

So a direct response to the question Holly had posed to me years before of "What are you going to do with your life?" was that with my new role that was taking me back to high school, I would be spending my time to make possible the next wave of Chris Gardners. And when I refer to the next Chris Gardners, let's point out that this includes GIRLS!

Brooke is leading that charge. Much as I expected, she mastered the harmonica and moved on to the drums. How good is she? Only time and her own permission to dream will tell. On the basketball court, Honey Bear has long ago surpassed "One hand, one foot." Recently she told me there was a star center on another team she'd been hearing about. Before I could say a word, Brooke said to me, "Well, when we play them next, she'll be hearing about me."

Whenever her plans to run for the presidency one day are raised, Brooke is quick to say that she's working on her world-class skills toward that end.

One of the joys of my job right now is that I also am able to work with community leaders, corporate executives, organizations, and institutions to create opportunities for all who are choosing to give themselves permission to dream. Early in my tour, after speaking at the An Achievable Dream Academy in Newport News, Virginia, I met a young lady, thirteen years of age and in the seventh grade. She approached me confidently and said, "Mr. Gardner, my dream is to be a chemical engineer and work for NASA!" Her question was whether that could be done; she needed reassurance. Why? Because she worried that when the time came she would need to forego her dream and help her family by going to work at a job that didn't require a higher education degree.

I had no doubt when I reassured her, "That can be done!" My confidence came from the fact that my foundation had already formed a partnership with NASA. Program leaders have agreed that every teaching tool and all the bells and whistles—currently used to encourage curiosity in science, technology, engineering arts, and mathematics in colleges and universities all over the world—will be made available to middle school and high school students for the first time on our platform.

The lesson I've learned from going Back 2 High School is that dreams need hope to become real. Hope should be given with love, freely, yet with reality checks built in.

Holly clearly knew what she was doing by challenging me to give myself my own permission to dream. My JFK moment—which, by the way, I think is more necessary than ever for all of us—has led to some of my greatest experiences of joy. It's a composite of all my dreams.

For any of you who have ever felt that you've reached a pinnacle in your life that you can never top, think again. That's not living or achieving the masterpiece life you have within you to create. Ask not how your dream is going to benefit you, ask how your dream can benefit the world.

We are living right now in what Holly insisted should be seen as Atomic Time. None of us knows how many days or months or years we have left, especially not in the 2020s. So you have to make every moment count. You have to create your masterpiece life You have to paint your Sistine Chapel. Back 2 High School has been that for me.

Oddly enough, a short while after the B2HS launch I found out that Holly hadn't been just seeing something inaccurately. Turns out there are these super-intricate, high-tech devices known as atomic clocks. These clocks were invented to measure as close as possible the exact length of a second—which is understood by all the masters of timekeeping to be the base unit for measuring time. Everywhere in the world, across all national, cultural, and language barriers, the universally accepted definition of a second is the time required for 9,192,631,770 (or nine billion plus) oscillations of a cesium 133 atom. The atomic oscillations are not so different from the swinging pendulum in a grandfather clock—only they are a billion times more precise.

Atomic Time right now can be the scariest part of your life, the most challenging part of your life, and the most transformational time of your masterpiece life if you're willing to let your dreams guide you. That's something I felt even before the world went upside down in March of 2020 and everything came to a screeching halt. In the middle of a terrifying deadly onslaught of a global pandemic accompanied by a worldwide financial crash, here in the United States we had a tragic lack of leadership. At the same time, the entire country witnessed the killing of unarmed Black citizens by police and others that has led to a protest and change movement—with the most mobilized numbers of citizens ever to say "enough is enough." Systemic racism and white supremacy were now under the spotlight and finally being addressed.

Beyond killing us, COVID-19 has laid bare a host of pre-existing conditions that many of us did not want to acknowledge. Some examples: 1. Racism is a pre-existing condition. 2. Sexism is a pre-existing condition. 3. Misogyny is a pre-existing condition. 4. Income inequality is a pre-existing condition. 5. Xenophobia is a pre-existing condition.

Just as it will be up to scientists and public health experts to solve this deadly, highly contagious airborne virus, it is going to be up to those of us who can dream and do to seek cures for our pre-existing conditions. We must cure those ills for our survival.

In the most practical terms, we have to change. Certainly, Covid-19 has radically altered how we work and where we work. For me, used to traveling and speaking every other day on average in front of thousands, this was a hard pivot to try to speak virtually. It was a crazy hard pivot for teachers, schools, and students.

The quiet and solitude of quarantine has required a different kind of hard pivot. For a few months people started reading more, getting out and walking more, with less rushing here and there. And in that pivoting, in these days of Atomic Time, we have had to dream anew. Not just to get by but also to imagine Beyond the Wall, beyond our fears, what a masterpiece life might look like for everyone.

On my days of worrying, I have been deeply alarmed by the rising numbers of the working homeless and the displaced. Yet I keep hearing from young activists who are not afraid, who are stepping up, who are marching, who are becoming the dreamers and the doers—the cavalry we need right now. They are shaping the new dream, they are defining the substance of masterpiece lives, and they are taking us to the next Promised Land. They invite all of us to join them.

Within the classrooms that have been part of B2HS, in person and now virtually, I have to say that the stories, questions, dreams, and convictions that I've encountered in this up-and-coming generation of young people give me tremendous hope. They are fearless. They don't carry the baggage of their parents or grandparents, even though they have inherited a heavier load to carry than any generation in the past one hundred years.

Atomic Time, no question, requires a hard pivot just to earn a living. Nothing about this is easy. Yet we have a choice as to where we put our energies and whose spiritual genetics we embrace.

We are pivoting away from the old paradigm of *doing and having* as we enter a period when what counts more are the values of *being and becoming*. The late Nelson Mandela, whose friendship and mentorship I was so fortunate to have, once said that our generation—from the baby boomers to the Y's and the millennials to the Z's—will be the ones who will rise by being about something bigger than ourselves. Our masterpiece lives will come from taking on causes fully and allowing ourselves to be fully engaged to the nth degree in the passionate and collaborative pursuit of our new vision of the American Dream. The same goes for other countries who seek to reenvision the Universal Dream where they live, work, and interact with one another.

A new vision of the American Dream, I believe, must be as bold as the vision of the founding fathers and mothers, appreciative of today's challenges but clearly focused on the future. This vision should be one of empowerment, not entitlement, and a reminder that we should no longer confuse net worth with self-worth. A new vision would help us see that achieving balance in our lives is as important as the balance in our checking accounts. In this new paradigm for the American Dream, we'll come to understand that the freedom to do, be, and have all that we dream must be tempered with the understanding that what we do does not define who we are. A new vision would come with the caveat that even though we dream of a day when we have all that we desire for ourselves and those we love, not all of what we desire is necessary for us to be happy. And I will further submit to you that however we collectively choose to define this new vision of the American Dream, it must have three components: a cornerstone, a backbone, and a bedrock. And do you know what that amounts to? The permission to dream. One hand, one foot!

* * *

The gift of Atomic Time came to me during one of my last public-speaking events before the lockdown began in March 2020. I was in Spain and speaking to thousands of mostly young adults in the most beautiful, resonant auditorium I'd ever experienced, and someone had brought their little girl to hear me speak. When we began the Q&A section at the end of my presentation, she went to the microphone and asked her question in Spanish, which was translated for me.

Her question was "What would you ask God?"

I thought about it, and the best answer I could give was "That is a big question. It is not *the* question. *The* question is what is God going to ask you?"

Whatever you perceive God to be, that question is important. Throughout the crowd I saw heads nodding vigorously. God might say something along the lines of "Look, I might not have given you everything you needed or deserved, but did you do everything you could have with what I did give you?"

This was now a question I was asking myself. More heads were nodding.

God might continue: "I gave you the same brain that I gave Albert Einstein. I know what he did with his. What did you do with yours? I gave you the same heart that I gave Mother Teresa. I know how she loved. How did you love? I gave you the same two arms that I gave Nelson Mandela. Who did you reach out to and who did you hold? I gave you the same two legs that I gave to a couple of guys—one who used his to walk on the moon and the other who used his to moonwalk. What did you do with your legs?"

There was a sudden stillness in the crowd. We were on the eve of a dark and uncertain time globally, but everyone looked excited to hear these questions.

This was the most important one of all, I thought: "I gave you the same two feet that I gave to everyone, so the question to you is, where did you stand, what did you stand for, and who did you stand with?"

With your permission to dream, let those questions be your guide. What will you do with what you have been given? How will you create your masterpiece life?

BRUSH YOUR TEETH AND CHANGE YOUR LIFE IN TWO DAYS

Back in the days when the parameters for B2HS were still being drawn up, I kept my promise to Brooke to visit Massachusetts and speak to her class about *Permission to Dream* and everything we had learned from each other on our expedition Beyond the Wall. The joy of being a grandparent, as others have pointed out to me, is in part how it gives you a second chance at doing things you might have done better as a parent. We had a pizza party with her whole class, and we talked about the basics—how little dreams become bigger ones, that sort of thing.

The students in her then-fifth-grade class wanted to know if the principles of dreaming were true for all ages. They wanted to know if they, their older siblings, their parents and grandparents, could use the same two questions I had used to find my dreams: *What do you do?* and *How do you do it?*

"Definitely," I assured them. As we talked, though, I realized that the time had come to update the two questions with newer, fresher ones.

Something else occurred to me too. Throughout childhood and adolescence I always envisioned *one day* as far off in the hard-to-read future. Even at my age, I know that for me and other grown-ups, it can feel at times that getting up the mountain is going to take *forevverrrrr.* Some change does take a long time. But I had just discovered it was possible to change my life in two days.

The thought occurred to me—what if there was a way to ask two new questions that would transform *one day* into today?

And what if these questions involved something we do every single day?

My answer nearly hit me upside the head. Here's what I proposed, and I need to let you know that this idea is so powerful that it has instigated a dental hygiene movement that's spreading out across the nation.

Very simply, you can do this once a day or even twice. Whenever you brush your teeth—*thoroughly,* I might add, and be sure to look at yourself in the mirror—my recommendation is that you start with permission to dream. You might think about your masterpiece life, your Sistine chapel, your This Page/That Page, your most audacious goals or whatever makes you feel happy, motivated, and so excited that you don't even want to go to bed because tomorrow can't get here fast enough.

Then ask yourself the first of two questions:

1. If tomorrow I could wake up and be or do anything what would it be?

Once you've determined what that would look like, smell like, feel like, and have engaged all of your senses in answering this question, move on to the second question.

2. What did I do today that will lead to that tomorrow?

That's right. Remember all the tips and tools. We are talking baby steps. Did you work on your 3R's, think about your blueprint, do an inventory of what's in your tackle box? Just as little dreams lead to big dreams, don't forget that little actions lead to big successes.

These two new questions are not only for kids—I promise. This exercise is applicable to all who need to be lifted, enriched, and empowered. Nobody is too far along to stop dreaming. Time to take a page from the book of Michelangelo, who at eighty-seven was quoted as saying that he was still learning and getting the hang of the whole art thing. There is no expiration date on the need to dream.

You may be skeptical, so let me tell you now about the Miracle

Question. This comes from a school of psychology called Solution Focused Therapy. Patients are asked to think about what a miracle could do to improve their lives if one occurred in the middle of the night after they went to sleep. They're asked to turn their problems over to the power of dreams to solve whatever their major issues, needs, and/or wants might be. Therapists who practice this approach then ask patients to consider ahead of time what their lives might be like in vivid detail if a miracle took place in the middle of the night.

The psychology of the Miracle Question and the Change Your Life in Two Days brushing your teeth program is one and the same. Dreams cause miracles. BAM.

That is where I leave you. That is the gift Holly wanted me to discover. When you dream of your miracle and ask what you want it to do for you, at the same time you are asking yourself what you can do to create the reality of that miracle. You then have all dreaming bases covered. We don't understand all the miracles, mysteries, and different forms of everyday magic that happen on a constant basis. We don't have all the answers. But what we do have is the choice to live in our seconds, in our moments, and in our limited time in the world. We do have a choice as to how we use all that has been given to us.

I will leave you with a favorite movie quote that might help you while you brush your teeth. The movie *Pretty Woman* is from back in the day—yeah, I said it—and the quote is from the last lines of the film, spoken by a character known as Happy Man, who, I'll never forget, says in a voiceover as credits roll, "Welcome to Hollywood! What's yo' dream?" And then, not at all sarcastically, he adds, "Keep on dreamin'."

You don't have to go to Hollywood to find dreams—trust me. Dreams do not have borders. Someone reading this right now already knows that. And if you don't, or if you aren't already dreamin', give yourself permission to do so. Right now.

Begin by answering this Happy Man's question to you: "What's yo' dream?"

ACKNOWLEDGMENTS

For anyone who thinks that a book is creatively conceived and then enjoyably written in one's leisure time before being sent off to publishers who bundle it all up and then deliver it to eager book buyers by stork, well, that is just obviously foolish.

C'mon, storks? We all know that storks don't deliver babies or books—angels do.

Permission to Dream would never have come to be if not for a handful of angels we wish to acknowledge first and foremost. Heartfelt thanks go to our agents, Jennifer Gates of Aevitas Creative Management, and Elizabeth Kaplan of the Elizabeth Kaplan Literary Agency. We are forever grateful to you both for your meaningful insights, your patience, and your unwavering support.

Endless gratitude goes to our editor and chief champion, Tracy Sherrod, book angel and fairy godmother. Thank you for your vision, your sense of the story and structure, and for putting the power of dreaming to the test in your own life. You waved your wand and sent us on a wonderful writing journey. This is the book we'd been dreaming to write. Thank you, Tracy.

We are so grateful for everyone on the team of our publishing home at HarperOne/Amistad. Special thanks to our rock star publisher Judith Curr, and to our key players, Courtney Nobile, publicist, and Emily Strode, production editor.

As always, I want to thank the team that works with me to keep me on task every day. A very special THANK YOU to Tina T and Solly Dolly—without the two of whom there would be chaos in Happyness!

And THE most heartfelt THANK YOU to Mim Eichler Rivas—my personal muse and in-house SHRINK! Mim makes the BLENDER WORK!

Mim has insisted on writing an acknowledgement that comes from her alone. She writes, "Collaborating with Chris Gardner (we're now on our third book) has been a dream come true. He is like having your own personal genie in the room. On his feet, he is a spectacular storyteller—thoughtful, authentic, hilarious, and soulful. And he can write like Miles Davis can play the trumpet. He is an angel to more people than he'll admit. He is never happier than when you've applied some of his wisdom to achieve a dream you'd never attempted before. Thank you to infinity, CG."

We want to express our sincere gratitude to everyone here in the United States who showed up on our election day and proved that democracy is alive and well, even after some battering. We dreamed of new leadership and gave ourselves permission to change course—as our founding fathers and mothers would have had us do. Toward the ideals of life, liberty, and the pursuit of happyness, our work is not done. We have to continue to dream and then act on those dreams together.

Most of the writing of *Permission to Dream* took place during the early months of the shutdown from the global pandemic of COVID-19 that has ravaged the world, especially here in the United States where numbers of cases and deaths are disproportionately, tragically high. We would be remiss if we didn't thank all the essential workers in every field of endeavor, particularly our medical and health care providers. You are our heroes. We dream of a nation that comes together to overcome all of our divides— and that is worthy of your sacrifices.

Finally, we want to again acknowledge readers and dreamers who come from every place on the planet. You summoned this book into being. Thank you.

SOURCES

CHAPTER 4. THE POWER OF ONE

Greta Thunberg, page 71. On climate change. https://www.youtube
.com/watch ?v=M7dVF9xylaw.

CHAPTER 5. CHANGE THE GAME

Warren Buffet, page 93. On my mentor, Ace Greenberg. Alan
C. Greenberg, Memos from a Chairman (New York: Workman
Publishing, 1996).

Percentage of Fortune 500 corporations founded in recessions,
page 99. On finding hidden opportunity. www.huffpost.com/entry
/top-companies-started-during-a-recession_n_923853.

ABOUT THE AUTHORS

Chris Gardner is the CEO of Happyness. In addition to being the author of two *New York Times* and international bestselling books, Gardner has also won a Peabody Award as a producer for *And Still I Rise*, the documentary based on the life of his friend and mentor, Dr. Maya Angelou. Since retiring from the financial services business after a thirty-five-year career, Mr. Gardner has maintained a pace as an internationally sought-after speaker that is unrivalled. Through the work of the Christopher P. Gardner Foundation, he's been able to connect with hundreds of thousands of students all across America. Gardner is currently a major investor in private equity—with a focus on cyber-security and asset management. Chris resides in Chicago and is learning Arabic.

Mim Eichler Rivas has worked as an author, coauthor, and collaborator on more than three dozen books, including the *New York Times* bestsellers *The Pursuit of Happyness* and *Finding Fish*. Several of her works have become feature films. She is the author of the highly acclaimed *Beautiful Jim Key*. Mim lives in Hermosa Beach, California, and dances hip-hop.